THE CAMBRIDGE BIBLE COMMENTARY

NEW ENGLISH BIBLE

General Editors: P. R. ACKROYD, A. R. C. LEANEY, J. W. PACKER

THE MAKING OF
THE OLD TESTAMENT

EDITED BY

ENID B. MELLOR

Lecturer in Religious Education
University of London Institute of Education

CAMBRIDGE
AT THE UNIVERSITY PRESS
1972

Published by the Syndics of the Cambridge University Press
Bentley House, 200 Euston Road, London NW1 2DB
American Branch: 32 East 57th Street, New York, N.Y. 10022

© Cambridge University Press 1972

Library of Congress Catalogue Card Number: 71-163063

ISBNS:
0 521 08184 X clothbound
0 521 09673 1 paperback

Printed in Great Britain
at the University Printing House, Cambridge
(Brooke Crutchley, University Printer)

GENERAL EDITORS' PREFACE

The aim of this series is to provide commentaries and
other books about the Bible, based on the text of the New
English Bible, and in these various volumes to make
available to the general reader the results of modern
scholarship. Teachers and young people have been
especially kept in mind. The commentators have been
asked to assume no specialized theological knowledge,
and no knowledge of Greek or Hebrew. Bare references
to other literature and multiple references to other parts of
the Bible have been avoided. Actual quotations have
been given as often as possible.

The completion of the New Testament part of the
series in 1967 provides a basis upon which the production
of the much larger Old Testament and Apocrypha series
can be undertaken. The welcome accorded to the series
has been an encouragement to the editors to follow the
same general pattern, and an attempt has been made to
take account of criticisms which have been offered.

The series is accompanied by three volumes of a more
general character, designed to provide in somewhat
greater detail the background information which is
needed for the study of the books of the Old Testament
and which can only be sketched in very brief form in the
separate commentary volumes. This one, *The Making of
the Old Testament*, is concerned with the formation of the
books of the Old Testament and Apocrypha in the context of the ancient Near Eastern world, and with the
ways in which these books have come down to us in
the life of the Jewish and Christian communities. Its
companion, *Understanding the Old Testament*, sets out to

provide the larger historical and archaeological background, to say something about the life and thought of the people of the Old Testament, and to answer the question 'Why should we study the Old Testament?'. The third volume, *Old Testament Illustrations*, contains maps, diagrams and photographs with an explanatory text. These three volumes are designed to provide material helpful to the understanding of the individual books and their commentaries, but they are also prepared so as to be of use quite independently.

P. R. A.

A. R. C. L.

J. W. P.

EDITOR'S PREFACE

The editor wishes to express gratitude to the other contributors to the volume and to the General Editors of the series for their help; also to the Reverend W. W. Simpson, O.B.E., M.A., of the Council of Christians and Jews, and to Mr Martin Cooper of the Jewish National Fund Education Department, for advice and guidance concerning chapter 6.

A. A. Macintosh (chapter 5) wishes to thank J. A. Crook, F.B.A., for many valuable suggestions, and Mrs V. Collis for help with the diagram and map on pp. 140 and 157.

E. B. M.

CONTENTS

2 THE POETRY AND PROSE OF THE OLD TESTAMENT

By *Enid B. Mellor*

3 OTHER WRITINGS OF THE JEWISH COMMUNITY

By *Margaret Barker*

CONTENTS

6 THE OLD TESTAMENT FOR JEWS AND CHRISTIANS TODAY
By *Enid B. Mellor*

ILLUSTRATIONS

1

THE LITERATURES OF THE ANCIENT NEAR EAST

Ancient Israel was a buffer state between her two great neighbours, Egypt and Mesopotamia. She was exposed to their ways and ideas, and vulnerable also to invasion, so that her land was for centuries the home of other nations and cultures.

If we are to begin to understand the Old Testament story of Israel we must try to assess to what extent it is bound up historically, culturally and religiously with the literature of Israel's neighbours. Fortunately there is plenty of information to help us, for during the past century archaeological discovery has brought to life this part of the ancient world, making our first problem one of selection. Documents from further afield, such as those relating to Crete, Greece and Asia Minor, cannot begin to be examined here, and of the evidence available from Canaan and the surrounding nations only a fraction can be considered. The choice has been made in an attempt to cover as wide a range as possible, both in time and in type of literature, and in the hope that it may serve as an introduction to further study of the Old Testament in its setting.

THE LITERATURE OF MESOPOTAMIA

Mesopotamia, meaning 'the land between the rivers', is the name given in the Greek Old Testament to the Tigris and Euphrates valleys and the country between them – traditionally from time to time the home of the

I

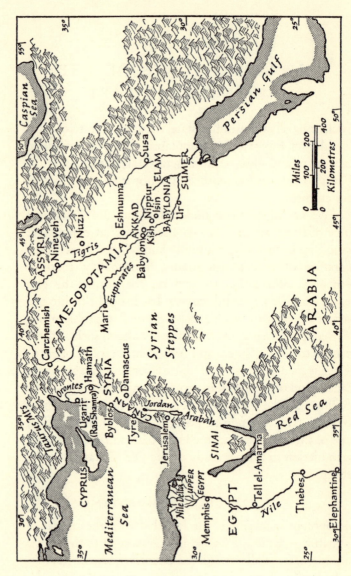

1. The Near East in Old Testament times

2

Patriarchs, Abraham and his descendants down to Joseph. During Old Testament times this land, or parts of it, was invaded and conquered by the Sumerians, Akkadians, Amorites, Assyrians, Chaldaeans and Persians, to name only some of the nations who made their homes there. The northern part of the area is also often referred to geographically as Assyria and the southern as Babylonia, regardless of whether or not there was at the time an independent kingdom of Assyria or Babylonia. 'Assyria' is derived from the name of a people, 'Babylonia' from her chief city, Babylon.

Politically speaking, Babylonia's first time of greatness, frequently called Old Babylon, was from about 1830 to 1550 B.C. Assyria began to emerge towards the end of this period, but came to the height of her power much later, from 883 to 612 B.C., after which she was subdued by the Chaldaeans. They set up the kingdom of 'Neo-Babylon', which flourished until 539 B.C., when it was absorbed into the empire of Cyrus the Persian. These were the Meso-potamian kingdoms which had most to do with Israel; they and other ancient powers of the Near East are listed in the chronological table on p. 4.

The method of writing employed in Mesopotamia was known as cuneiform, meaning 'wedge-shaped'. Invented by the Sumerians, who settled in the south from about 4000 B.C., it consisted of impressions upon clay made by a wedge-shaped stylus, or, for permanent, monumental work, of carving upon stone. Sometimes writing-boards were used; made of wood or ivory, they had an inlay of wax mixed with coloured substance, soft enough to take the impression of a stylus. These boards had two advan-tages: they could be hinged together and folded flat to give any length of writing surface, and their inlay

Date B.C.	Mesopotamia	Syria-Palestine	Egypt
			Wisdom of Ptah-hotep (about 2450)
2400 ►	Archaeological findings are underlined		
2300 ►			OLD KINGDOM (2686 –2160)
2200 ►	Laws of Ur Nammu (2050)		
2100 ►	Creation and Flood Epics (about 2000)		
2000 ►	Laws of Kingdom of Eshnunna (about 2000)		MIDDLE KINGDOM (2160 –1786)
1900 ►	Laws of Lipit Ishtar of Isin (1950–1900)		Execration Texts (1900–1700)
1800 ►	OLD KINGDOM OF BABYLON (1830–1550)	PROLONGED PERIOD OF EGYPTIAN RULE	
1700 ►	Law Code of Hammurabi (1728–1686) Mari Tablets (about 1690)		RULE OF HYKSOS (1750–1568)
1600 ►			
1500 ►	Nuzi Tablets (1500–1400)		NEW KINGDOM (1568–1085)
1400 ►		Ras Shamra Tablets (about 1400)	
1300 ►	DECLINE OF BABYLON AND RISE OF ASSYRIA	Tell el-Amarna Tablets (1400–1360)	Teaching of Amen-em-opet (1300)
1200 ►		Settlement in Canaan (1250–1200)	The Exodus (about 1280)
1100 ►		PERIOD OF THE JUDGES (1200–1020)	
1000 ►		UNITED MONARCHY (1020 –922)	
900 ►		Death of Solomon (922) Division of Kingdom	PERIOD OF DECLINE (1085 –525)
800 ►	ASSYRIAN EMPIRE (883–612)	JUDAH ISRAEL Moabite Stone (830)	
700 ►	Babylonian Chronicle (626–539)	Fall of Samaria to Assyria (722) 1st Fall of Jerusalem (597)	
600 ►	Jehoiachin Tablets (595–570) NEO-BABYLON (612–539)	Lachish Letters (590-588) 2nd Fall of Jerusalem (586)	Conquest by Persia (525)
500 ►	Cyrus Cylinder (539)	1st Return of Exiles (539)	Elephantine Papyri (495–400)
400 ►	PERSIAN RULE 539–333	Nehemiah (444) Ezra (398)	End of Persian Rule (404)
300 ►	GREEK CONQUEST 333		

2. Table of dates

4

remained soft, so that alterations were easy. During the past hundred years thousands of cuneiform tablets have been excavated which have helped us to know more not only of 'the land between the rivers' and her history and religion, but also of her neighbours, including ancient Israel.

The Creation and Flood Stories

Ashurbanipal, king of Assyria from 668 to 633 B.C., was a cruel and ruthless military campaigner and at the same time a man of culture, who according to one of his own inscriptions 'learned the wisdom of Nabu, the entire art of writing on clay tablets'. From his capital at Nineveh he sent scribes throughout Mesopotamia to copy and translate into Akkadian, the language of Assyria and Babylonia, the documents they found, and to bring them back to the royal palace. A very considerable library resulted, which was unearthed partly in A.D. 1853 by Hormuzd Rassam, partly in 1873–6 by George Smith, a young assistant at the British Museum who had deciphered some of the tablets found earlier and discovered that they told the story of a great flood, not unlike that of Genesis. George Smith's excavations brought to light thousands more tablets, 'giving', as he wrote to the *Daily Telegraph*, 'the history of the world from the Creation to the Fall of Man'.

Although most of these texts were written down in Ashurbanipal's time, and none of them earlier than 1000 B.C., they were originally composed in Old Babylon, perhaps as early as 2000 B.C. Yet even this is not the beginning of the story. Subsequent to the discoveries at Nineveh, excavations at Nippur and Kish have shown that the Sumerians also knew and recorded these traditions of Creation, Paradise and a great flood. No doubt when the Semitic invaders (from whom came most of the later inhabitants of Mesopotamia) took over the Sumerians' style of writing, they also inherited some of their religious traditions.

The keynote of the *Creation Story* is conflict. Apsu and Tiamat, the gods of fresh water and salt water, are overcome and slain by their offspring, and the hero of the final victory is Marduk, who creates heaven and earth from the dead bodies of his opponents. As king of the gods Marduk makes man to be their servant, and builds Babylon as his home.

At first all this looks very different from Genesis, and indeed the whole behaviour of the gods, including Marduk's purpose in creating man, seems foreign to biblical thought. Yet there are similarities. The Babylonian myth begins:

When on high the heaven had not been named,
Firm ground below had not been called by name,

a setting not unlike the watery chaos of Gen. 1: 2, where 'the earth was without form and void', and continues with an order of creation which, leaving aside the rather major omissions of animals, fish and birds, roughly corresponds to that of Genesis 1. Then in Ps. 74: 13, 14 we read:

by thy power thou didst cleave the sea-monster in two
and break the sea-serpent's heads above the waters;
thou didst crush Leviathan's many heads
and throw him to the sharks for food.

So here, as elsewhere in the Old Testament (for example, Ps. 89: 10, Job 7: 12, Isa. 51: 9), there are references to a primaeval conflict, reminiscent of that between the gods of Babylon, but this time with Yahweh, the God of

6

Israel (for the derivation of the name see pp. 143, 160), defeating monsters called Leviathan, or Rahab, or 'the sea-serpent'.

In the *Flood Story*, which is part of a much longer poem called the *Epic of Gilgamesh*, the gods determine to destroy mankind. The hero, Utnapishtim, builds a ship, and with his family, animals and possessions survives. The ship grounds on Mount Nisir, and after seven days Utnapishtim sends out a dove which

Went forth but came back;
Since no resting place for it was visible, she turned round,

and this exercise is later repeated with a swallow and with a raven; the latter

went forth and, seeing that the waters had diminished,
He eats, circles, caws, and turns not round.

When the family leave the ship they offer sacrifice, and Utnapishtim is given immortality by the gods.

In recent years, further study of some of the fragmentary material in the Ashurbanipal tablets, together with other texts dating back to the reign of Ammisadduqa, who was king of Babylon some thousand years before Ashurbanipal reigned in Assyria, has shown that the source of this story was the Babylonian *Epic of Atrahasis*. The hero, like Utnapishtim, warned of coming judgement, escapes with family, animals and birds in a home-made (and rather simpler) boat, and, after a flood lasting seven days (the account of the grounding of the ship is missing), disembarks and offers sacrifice.

Here as in the *Creation Story* there are points of likeness to Genesis – amongst them the danger, the recording of the specification of the ship and the duration of the flood, and, in the Gilgamesh Epic, the grounding on a

7

mountain and the sending out of the birds. But there are major differences: the apparently capricious reason for the deluge, and the conferring of immortality on Utnapishtim, or, in the Atrahasis Epic, the description of a system of social class for the post-deluvian era, contrast sharply with the covenant between Yahweh and Noah described in Gen. 9: 12–17.

Obviously the writers of early Genesis knew their own forms of these ancient stories, elements of which indeed seem to have been known throughout the whole of the ancient Near East. Yet we must not overrate the connection. The use of traditional material does not necessarily imply an uncritical acceptance of its underlying ideas; the violent, unpredictable deities of Babylonia are far removed from the God of the Old Testament. If we read Genesis side by side with the Babylonian material it is difficult to escape the conclusion that they are founded upon widely differing religious ideas and principles.

Mari, Nuzi and the Age of the Patriarchs

Genesis chapters 12 to 50, the stories of Abraham, Isaac, Jacob, Joseph and his brothers, are not contemporary records; on any theory they are accepted as having been written hundreds of years after the events they claim to describe. None of the characters can be identified in history, nor can we place within centuries when they could have lived. Yet evidence from Mesopotamia, of the period roughly between 2000 and 1500 B.C., throws a certain light on these stories. Of this evidence perhaps the most interesting is the material discovered at Mari and Nuzi.

Somewhere around 2000 B.C. there was a great movement into the Near East of nomadic peoples who had lived on its outer fringes. These invaders, called

'Westerners', or 'Amorites', by the Babylonians, set up a number of independent states in and to the west of Mesopotamia. (In the Old Testament the Amorites are mentioned in Gen. 15: 16 as inhabiting the land of Canaan, and are included in the list of nations whom the Israelites were later instructed to drive out (Deut. 7: 1). They were defeated a number of times, but remnants survived until the tenth century B.C., when according to 1 Kings 9: 20, 21 Solomon incorporated them into his forced labour corps. After this they disappear from the biblical scene.)

In 1936 excavations directed by André Parrot, under the auspices of the Musée du Louvre, began on the upper Euphrates, and subsequently revealed *Mari*, capital of an Amorite kingdom which flourished until its last king, Zimri Lim, was defeated by Hammurabi of Babylon in about 1697 B.C. The royal palace of some three hundred rooms contained the royal archives, upwards of 20,000 clay tablets, about 5,000 of them communications to Zimri Lim from officials, local chiefs and neighbouring kings. In these records the names Levi and Israel occur, with others from the same roots as Gad and Dan – though without any reference to Old Testament characters or tribes. The king is worried by nomads on the fringe of the desert, and the most troublesome group is the Banu-Yamina (another form of Benjamin); one 'Bannum, the king's servant' reports:

Yesterday I departed from Mari, and spent the night at Zuruban. All the Banu-Yamina raised fire-signals...and so far I have not ascertained the meaning of those signals. Now, I shall determine the meaning, and I shall write to my lord whether it is thus or not. Let the guard of the city of Mari be strengthened, and let my lord not go outside the gate.

Nuzi, east of the Tigris and 150 miles north of Baghdad, was excavated between 1925 and 1931 by a joint expedition of the American School of Oriental Research in Baghdad, and Harvard University. It was the home of the Hurrians (the biblical Horites of Gen. 14: 6), and tablets of the fifteenth century B.C. (some of them now in the British Museum) reflect various customs of the time and may elucidate some of the incidents in Genesis. For instance, there are provisions for childless couples to provide themselves with an heir; they could adopt a son to look after them in old age and ensure a decent burial, as Abram apparently adopted Eliezer (Gen. 15: 2), but the bargain would be at least partly nullified by the birth of a son. In one case of an adopted son whose wife failed to produce children, it was decreed that she should give a handmaid to her husband, as Sarah gave Hagar (Gen. 16: 2), and Rachel, Bilhah (Gen. 30: 3). The 'tablet of adoption belonging to Nashwi', who adopted a certain Wullu, rules that 'If Nashwi has a son of his own he shall divide (the estate) equally with Wullu, but the son of Nashwi shall take the gods of Nashwi'. Obviously the possession of the household gods marked the legitimate heir, hence Laban's anxiety in Gen. 31: 26 ff. when he discovered Rachel's theft of his images. In the same tablet, Nashwi bids Wullu marry his (Nashwi's) daughter and none other: 'If Wullu takes another wife he shall forfeit the lands and buildings of Nashwi', just as Laban bound Jacob in Gen. 31: 50: 'If you ill-treat my daughters or take other wives beside them when no one is there to see, then God be witness between us.'

Once more, the value of such evidence must not be exaggerated. It helps us to understand, and within limits to date, the background of the patriarchal stories. But it cannot prove or disprove the people and events as history. Our knowledge of the lives of Abraham, Isaac and Jacob is confined to the biblical records, which lie beyond the scope of archaeological proof.

Law and the community

The oldest known collection of laws comes from Mesopotamia, and is dated perhaps as early as 2050 B.C. It is the work of *Ur Nammu*, self-styled 'king of Sumer and Akkad', who founded and presided over the splendid civilization of the Third Dynasty of Ur in southern Mesopotamia, traditionally the city of Abram's birth (Gen. 11:27–31). This Sumerian code, discovered among texts in the Museum of the Ancient Orient at Istanbul, tells how the god Nanna chose Ur Nammu to rule as his representative, and how the latter got rid of dishonest and profiteering officials and established a reliable system of weights and measures. The few actual laws which survive seem to be concerned to prevent victimization and protect the rights of the individual; certain fines are imposed upon those who injure others.

Belonging probably to the late twentieth century B.C. are two tablets (now in the Iraq Museum) discovered near Baghdad on the site of a town in the ancient *kingdom of Eshnunna*, and recording in Akkadian the laws of that kingdom. The preamble states that Tishpak, god of Eshnunna, has appointed the king, whose name is lost but who is tentatively identified with Bilalama, who reigned round about 1920 B.C. Some sixty paragraphs of regulations, mainly concerned with property, follow. For example: 'If an ox is known to gore habitually and...it gores a man and causes (his death), then the owner of the ox shall pay two-thirds of a mina of silver.'

Further south, and a little later, in the early nineteenth century B.C., *King Lipit Ishtar* ruled over the *kingdom of Isin*, and promulgated yet another code of laws, written, like that of Ur Nammu, in Sumerian, perhaps because it derived from an earlier Sumerian heritage. (Some of these tablets are now in the Louvre, but most are in the Museum of the University of Pennsylvania.) Once again the king begins by claiming the authority of the gods, and continues by legislating for such situations as a man renting an ox and damaging it, in which case he must pay a proportionate part of the ox's price, according to the damage.

More famous and more complete than these older codes is that of *Hammurabi*, king of Babylon between 1728 and 1686 B.C., whom we have already met as the conqueror of Zimri Lim of Mari. Discovered in 1901 at Susa, a city to the east of Babylon, the six-foot-high tablet of black diorite on which one copy of the code is inscribed now stands in the Louvre. The Akkadian text begins with the now-familiar prologue attributing the king's authority to the gods, and ends with a long epilogue summing up Hammurabi's hopes that justice will be done and that the oppressed will understand their rights – and, incidentally, will give credit where it is due by saying, 'Hammurabi, the lord, who is like a real father to the people, bestirred himself for the word of Marduk, his lord...'

The legal provisions themselves, almost three hundred of them, cover commercial, social, domestic and moral procedure. Some are obviously based on earlier codes; for instance the rules regarding the dangerous ox and the damage to a hired animal, already quoted from Eshnunna and Lipit Ishtar of Isin, make their reappearance. From this and from the similarity in arrangement (prologue, provisions mainly using the 'casuistic' or case-law formula, 'If a man...then...', and epilogue), it seems that from early times Mesopotamia had a fairly standard legal system for use in dealing with its numerous and complex communities.

The *Laws of Israel*, though written later, show evidence of a common background. The code known as the Book of the Covenant (Exod. 20: 22 – 23: 33) begins with a historical and theological prologue: 'The Lord said to Moses, "Say this to the Israelites: You know now that I have spoken to you from heaven..."' Many of the provisions that follow are in the casuistic form, 'When (or if) it should happen...' and the epilogue (Exod. 23: 20-33) contains warnings and promises of the consequences of disobedience and obedience. There are similarities in content as well as in form: for instance the *Lex talionis* ('Law of a tooth') of Exod. 21: 23-5, 'Eye for eye, tooth for tooth, hand for hand...', has its parallel in Hammurabi's principle of retaliation: 'If a seignior has knocked out a tooth of a seignior of his own rank, they shall knock out his tooth.' ('Seignior' translates the Akkadian *awelum*, a free citizen, usually of some standing.)

There are, however, underlying divergences. The overriding concern of the Mesopotamian systems is with property; that of the Law of Israel with people. In the former there is a preponderance of laws dealing with possessions over those dealing with persons; in the Old Testament the reverse is the case. This difference in emphasis is also reflected in the penalties imposed. According to the codes of Eshnunna and Hammurabi, the man whose ox gores someone to death is to pay a fine. Exod. 21: 29 cites the same situation, but 'the ox shall be stoned, and the owner shall be put to death as well'. The severity of the biblical punishment reflects a graver view of an offence which caused a death.

Nor are all the laws in the Pentateuch (the name given to the first five Old Testament books, from the Greek *pente* = 'five', *teuchos* = 'book') cast in the conventional casuistic mould; some, notably the Ten Commandments, are 'apodictic' in form – that is, categorical commands or prohibitions, without conditions and without indication as to how they are to be implemented. This form, much more akin to the 'These are the words of the Lord' of the prophets, is rare elsewhere in ancient Near Eastern law, though there are parallels particularly in the Hittite treaties between king and vassal. In law, as in mythology, Israel was aware of and influenced by her environment, yet in the deepest sense independent of it.

Historical records: the Babylonian and Persian view of the fall of Jerusalem, exile and return

The Babylonian Chronicle

In 626 B.C. the Chaldaeans seized Babylon and established the Neo-Babylonian empire, thus constituting an active threat to Assyria, who as the dominant Near Eastern power had swallowed up the Northern Kingdom of Israel in 722 B.C. The story of Neo-Babylon's greatness and of her fall in 539 B.C. was recorded in the Babylonian Chronicle, a year by year account of events and conquests. Some of these records survive and are in the British Museum; inevitably they overlap in places with the Old Testament story of the same era.

In 612 B.C. Nineveh, the Assyrian capital, fell to the Babylonians and Medes, and in 605 B.C. Babylon consolidated her position by decisively defeating the Egyptian army at Carchemish, Egypt's base on the upper Euphrates. From now on there are yearly accounts of sorties into 'the land of Hatti' (Syria–Palestine), and in 604 B.C. the new king, Nebuchadnezzar, 'Took the heavy tribute of the Hatti-land back to Babylon', presumably including that of king Jehoiakim of Judah, who switched allegiance from Egypt to Babylon and so for the time being avoided his country's complete overthrow (2 Kings 24: 1).

Three years later Nebuchadnezzar pushed on into Egypt to confront the army of Pharaoh Necho II, and the Chronicle honestly admits heavy losses on both sides. The Babylonian army returned home and remained there for eighteen months, and possibly this setback inspired Jehoiakim to stop paying tribute. The Chronicle takes up the story with an account of Nebuchadnezzar's reprisals against Jerusalem:

in the seventh year, in the month of Kislev, the Babylonian king mustered his troops, and having marched to the land of Hatti, besieged the city of Judah, and on the second day of the month of Adar took the city and captured the king. He appointed therein a king of his own choice, received its heavy tribute and sent (them) to Babylon.

This is the first fall of Jerusalem, recorded in 2 Kings 24: 1–17. A comparison of the accounts reveals substantial agreement; the captured king is the young Jehoiachin, who was taken to Babylon together with '(his) mother and his wives, his eunuchs and the foremost men of the land' (2 Kings 24: 15). The 'king of (Nebuchadnezzar's) own choice' is Mattaniah, whose name was changed to Zedekiah as a sign of subjection, and the 'heavy tribute' sent to

Babylon would include the treasures from the temple and palace. The Babylonian story gives a further piece of information in that it dates the fall of the city precisely as the 'second day of the month of Adar', which has been calculated as 16 March 597 B.C.

The Jehoiachin Tablets

The surviving texts of the Babylonian Chronicle do not cover the final fall of Jerusalem in 586 B.C., but other records tell us something of the fortunes of Jehoiachin after his capture and deportation in 597 B.C. Stored in an underground building near Babylon's Ishtar Gate were some three hundred tablets, discovered between 1899 and 1917, and now in the Berlin Museum. They appear to have been the records of the official in charge of rations, and they account for the allotment of oil, barley and spices to craftsmen and captives. The names of the recipients, ranging in origin from Egypt to Persia and from Elam to Asia Minor, give us an idea of the cosmopolitan life of this city where the Jews were far from being the only foreigners, and included in the lists are names from Judah, such as Gaddiel, Shelemaiah and Semechaiah.

The most important allowance recorded is that given to 'Ya'ukinu king of the land of Yehudu', otherwise Jehoiachin king of Judah, and his family. From the treatment meted out to him it appears that Jehoiachin was regarded by the Babylonians as well as by the Jews as the legal claimant to the throne of Judah; it is therefore hardly surprising that Jewish writers of this period and after date events in terms of his years of exile (see Jer. 52: 31, Ezek. 1: 2, etc.). We know from 2 Kings 25: 27–8 that in the thirty-seventh year of his exile Jehoiachin was 'brought out of prison' by Evil-merodach, then king of

Babylon, but the royal ration card found near the Ishtar Gate is dated only five years after his deportation. Taking the two accounts together it would appear either that 'prison' for the king and his entourage was little more than house arrest, perhaps in the building where the tablets were found, or that in the early years he was free to move about the city, and that actual imprisonment only came later.

The Cyrus Cylinder

In 539 B.C. Babylon fell to Cyrus the Persian who, like all conquerors, found many things which he felt called for reorganization and reformation. His own account of this conquest, inscribed upon a clay cylinder (now in the British Museum), attributes the call to conquer to Marduk, the chief Babylonian god, who 'went at his side like a friend and comrade' and 'caused the big-hearted inhabitants of Babylon to (love?) him'. There is no specific mention of the liberation of the Jews, but, referring to the distant cities of the empire, Cyrus says, 'I gathered together all their inhabitants and restored (to them) their dwellings'; also, at the bidding of Marduk he re-dispersed the local gods which had been brought into Babylon and 'made (them) to dwell in peace in their habitations, delightful abodes'.

Despite these tributes to Marduk, the Old Testament writers see Cyrus as inspired by Yahweh. It is Yahweh who elects Cyrus (Isa. 44: 28, 45: 1), Yahweh who will 'go before (him)' (Isa. 45: 2), Yahweh who commissions him to rebuild Jerusalem and the temple (Isa. 44: 28, 45: 13). Above all, according to his Decree of Restoration recorded in Ezra 1: 1–11, Cyrus himself claims that 'The Lord the God of heaven has given me all the kingdoms of the earth, and he himself has charged me to build him a house at Jerusalem in Judah'.

The events recorded by the Cyrus Cylinder and the Old Testament are substantially the same, but the religious interpretations placed upon them are very different. The Jews saw their repatriation as the liberation of a subject people, the fulfilment by Yahweh's agent of Yahweh's promise. Cyrus, on the other hand, would have in mind his responsibilities to the whole of his newly-acquired territories and the need for propaganda which would dispose in his favour the Babylonians from whom these territories had been acquired. It was not surprising that in each case the literary result was the product of its own environment and couched in its own terms.

THE LITERATURE OF SYRIA—PALESTINE

Herodotus, writing in the fifth century B.C., refers to 'the part of Syria called Palestine'; elsewhere, more explicitly, he says, 'That part of Syria [i.e. the northern coast] and as much of it as reaches to Egypt, is called Palestine.' At that time the name 'Syria' meant all the fertile land bounded on the west by the Mediterranean Sea, on the south and east by desert, and on the north by the Taurus Mountains. In some versions of the English Old Testament, however, it is used to translate 'Aram' (1 Kings 19: 15, Isa. 7: 2, 8), the kingdom centring on Damascus in the north-eastern part of the larger area, home of the ancient Aramaean peoples, and scene of some of the patriarchal stories (Deut. 26: 5, Hos. 12: 12). In the New Testament Syria is a Roman province north and north-east of Galilee, and it is in fact in the more restricted northerly sense of the Old and New Testaments that the term is most usually understood.

The name 'Palestine', like Syria, is Greek in origin and derives from Philistia, the southern maritime plain on which the Philistines, immigrants from the Aegean, settled in about 1190 B.C., not long after the Israelites, their deadly rivals, had arrived from approximately the opposite direction. Although it was known to Herodotus, and later, in the first century B.C., to the Jewish historian Josephus, 'Palestine' as an official designation only came into use after A.D. 135: earlier, after the Israelite settlement in the thirteenth century B.C., it was called 'Israel' (Deut. 18: 6, 1 Sam. 13: 19). It has been said that the only certain boundary to Israel was the Mediterranean Sea in the west; ideally in the east it extended to 'the great river, the Euphrates' (Deut. 1: 7), but the more natural barrier was the deep rift valley of the River Jordan, running from north to south. Indeed, although the tribes settled on both sides of the river, Transjordan was often thought and spoken of as a separate area. The tribes of Reuben and Gad, laying claim to territory east of the river, are recorded as saying, 'We will claim no share of the land with them [the rest of the tribes] over the Jordan and beyond, because our patrimony has already been allotted to us east of the Jordan' (Num. 32: 19). The northern and southern limits are described variously as Dan and Beersheba (Judg. 20: 1) and as 'Lebohamath', or 'the entrance of Hamath' (probably the beginning of the valley between the Lebanon and anti-Lebanon mountains), and 'the Torrent of Egypt' (the Wadi el 'Arish, about half way between Gaza and the Suez Canal – see 1 Kings 8: 65).

Whether real or ideal, these limits enclosed a country of only 6,000 square miles, approximately the size of Wales – at most 145 miles long and 40 to 90 miles wide in its narrowest and broadest parts – plus the 4,000 square miles of Transjordan. Nor did the boundaries endure, for after the death of Solomon in 922 B.C. the land was divided into northern and southern kingdoms, known rather confusingly as 'Israel' and 'Judah'. Israel, the Northern Kingdom, was swallowed up by Assyria in 722 B.C. and deportees from other parts of the Assyrian empire were brought in, whilst the Southern Kingdom fell to Babylon in 586 B.C. It was to this latter area, re-named Judaea, that the Jews began to return from Babylon in 539 B.C., but Judaea was never again to be fully independent. She became part of the territories ruled successively by Persia, Greece, Egypt, Syria and Rome.

Syria–Palestine before the Conquest: the Tell el-Amarna and Ras Shamra tablets

Syria–Palestine's earliest name was Canaan, probably meaning 'land of the purple', with reference to the dye made from the murex shellfish found on the coast. This was the Promised Land of the Patriarchs (Gen. 15: 18, 19) and of the tribes under Moses and Joshua (Exod. 12: 25, Josh. 5: 6), and since before 3000 B.C. it had been popu-lated by peoples who, coming from outside, had become highly civilized. At the time of the Israelite conquest Canaan was at the end of a long period of (latterly nominal) Egyptian domination. Subsequently, pushed back by the Israelites from the south and east, the Philistines from the south and west and the Aramaeans from the north-east, her people retreated to the Lebanon mountains and the narrow coastal strip which they pro-tected. There, undaunted by decline and defeat, they cut down trees with their newly-invented iron axes, built ships, and became a great nation of traders and seafarers. Known as the Phoenicians (from the Greek *phoinix*, also meaning 'purple'), their capital was Tyre; their king Hiram I (969–936 B.C.) helped with materials and craftsmen for Solomon's temple (1 Kings 5: 7–12), which was possibly built to a Phoenician specification. They also exerted great influence on Greek culture, mainly through the trading centres which they established as far west as Spain, and not the least of their achievements was the invention of the first alphabetic (as opposed to pictorial) writing, which later spread to Greece and eventually to the whole known world.

The Israelites had much to learn from the people whom they dispossessed, whose dialect they 'took over', and whose architecture, literature and music they admired. Also, as will be seen, there was much that they needed to discard or even eradicate. Two of the main sources which help us to assess the extent of the assimilation of Canaanite traditions are the Tell el-Amarna letters, which describe the political conditions in the country before the Israelite conquest, and the Ras Shamra tablets, which do the same in the sphere of religion.

Most of the 378 texts known as the *Tell el-Amarna tablets* were found accidentally in 1877 by an Egyptian woman living near Amarna, about 200 miles south of Cairo; the beginning of a history of bargaining, sale and re-sale which has ended in the tablets being scattered all over the world from London to Leningrad and from Istanbul to Chicago. The bulk of them constitute an Egyptian Foreign Office file from the period somewhere between 1400 and 1360 B.C. This contains correspondence sent by rulers and officials of the Egyptian possessions in western Asia to the Pharaoh Amenhotep III and, more particularly, to his successor, Akhenaton, the brilliant, unconventional king who moved the capital from Thebes to Amarna, and introduced radical religious changes. Written in Akkadian, the chief language of Near Eastern diplomacy at the time, the letters were never intended for publication and are all the more fascinating for that. They reflect seething intrigues, jealousies and feuds between local governors, as well as details of politics, trade, commerce and warfare.

The correspondence from Canaan tells the same story as the rest, of external attack, internal strife among the vassal rulers of the city states, and lack of firm support and direction from Egypt. Rib-Addi, governor of Byblos in the north (biblical Gebal), wrote more than fifty letters in all, in one of which he says:

I have written repeatedly for garrison troops, but they were not given, and the king did not listen to the words of his servant. And I sent my courier to the palace, but he returned empty-handed – he had no garrison troops. And when the people of my house saw that silver was not given, they ridiculed me like the governors, my brethren, and they despised me.

In Megiddo the governor Biridiya, harassed by Lab'ayu, 'the lion-like', ruler of Shechem, writes: 'Ever since the archers returned to Egypt Lab'ayu has carried on hostilities against me. . . and now his face is set to take Megiddo, but let the king protect his city, lest Lab'ayu seize it.' Lab'ayu in turn protests spiritedly that he has been driven to this in self-defence: 'I am slandered/blamed before the King, my lord. Further, when even ants are smitten they do not accept it passively, but they bite the hand of the man who smites them. How could I hesitate this day when two of my towns are taken?'

For Old Testament study the tablets are of value in at least three respects. First, they throw some light on circumstances in Canaan not long before the Israelite settlement – a period on which the Old Testament is silent – and give us an idea of the conditions under weakening Egyptian suzerainty which no doubt helped to prepare the way for the Israelite conquest a century or more later.

Secondly, though more indirectly, they also give us glimpses of life in Egypt. In some of Rib-Addi's letters he mentions Yanhammu, an officer of the Egyptian court with considerable power in Canaan, one of whose duties it was to supply the subjects there with grain in times of scarcity. This and his Semitic name are reminiscent of Joseph, and, although Joseph and Yanhammu cannot be identified, these references show that it was not impossible for a Semite to attain a position of some influence under an Egyptian king.

Thirdly, and perhaps most significantly, the texts add to our information about the people called the Habiru. Six letters are from Abdi-Hiba of Jerusalem, who is menaced by these marauding bands and accuses some of his fellow rulers, notably the much-maligned Lab'ayu of Shechem, of making common cause with them. Writing to deny this, or rather to deny it on behalf of his son, who is the chief target for the accusations, Lab'ayu uses the term SA.GAZ for the Habiru, as also does Rib-Addi of Byblos; in other Egyptian texts the name 'Apiru almost certainly refers to the same group. The similarity between Habiru and 'Apiru is obvious; the link with SA.GAZ less so. The latter term may be a Sumerian ideograph (that is, a character which symbolizes the idea of something without expressing its name, rather like most Egyptian hieroglyphics), or it may mean 'plunderer', from the Akkadian *šāggašu*.

Who were the Habiru? The Tell el-Amarna tablets

describe them as bandits; at Mari in the eighteenth century B.C. they appear as mercenary soldiers; at Nuzi in the fifteenth century as household servants hiring themselves out under contract. From all this it seems that they were members of a social group, widespread over the ancient Near East, who could be hired as menials or soldiers, or who on occasion organized themselves into gangs as freebooters. Hardly surprisingly, the name Habiru came to be used generally of enemies or rebels.

Can we, then, connect or identify them with the Hebrews? A once-popular idea was that they were in fact the same, and that the Amarna texts were a Canaanite account of the invasion recorded in Joshua and early Judges, but archaeological evidence points with increasing unanimity to a thirteenth-century date for this entry, and makes the identification less than likely. Yet the Israelites are called Hebrews ('*Ibrim*, a word from a similar root to Habiru and 'Apiru) thirty-four times in the Old Testament, usually by foreigners or by themselves when speaking to foreigners, and certainly they spent much of their early history in nomadic wanderings. In the law codes, too, there are regulations for the treatment of 'Hebrew slaves' (Exod. 21: 2, Deut. 15: 12), and it seems possible that at one time 'Hebrew' was the correct social designation for a man sold as a slave. It may even have been that the term was originally used as an abusive nickname, and was then explained and rationalized in the Old Testament as coming from Eber, the ancestor of the race (Gen. 10: 24, 11: 14), whose name, from '*abar*, 'to cross over', is interpreted as 'him from beyond' (the River – that is, the Euphrates).

Perhaps the most that can be said is that the Old Testament Hebrews belonged to the widespread group for long known in general terms as the Habiru, but that there is no reason to identify them with any specific people mentioned in the Tell el-Amarna or other Near Eastern texts.

The *Ras Shamra texts* caused a sensation in the nineteen-thirties not unlike that made by the Dead Sea Scrolls in the forties and fifties. As with the Scrolls and the Tell el-Amarna tablets, the first discovery was by chance, made in 1928 by a peasant ploughing a field in northern Syria. The plough struck a large stone which was found to belong to a tomb-vault containing pottery. The following year an expedition led by C. F. A. Schaeffer, under the auspices of the Académie des Inscriptions et Belles-lettres, began the first of many seasons of excavation, interrupted only by the Second World War.

Near to the original tomb lay a great mound known as Ras Shamra, and beneath this Schaeffer discovered the remains of the Canaanite city of Ugarit. Mentioned in both the Mari and the Tell el-Amarna texts, Ugarit flourished until destroyed by earthquake in about 1360 B.C., then again, after rebuilding, until the twelfth century B.C. It was a cosmopolitan trading centre, and from about 1900 B.C. western influence was apparent in the form of distinctively Cretan pottery, Mycenean-type masonry, and installations similar to those attested in Crete and Cyprus, making provision for libations to the dead.

Adjoining one of the city's temples (built like that of Solomon on a tripartite plan of outer court with altar, inner court or hall, and inmost shrine), was a scribal library, containing a number of texts in a hitherto unknown script. This was alphabetic in form though written in cuneiform; within eighteen months of the discovery an alphabet of thirty characters was deciphered, and the name Ugaritic given to the new language. The texts, dated around 1400 B.C., and containing myth, saga and ritual (see pp. 46–7), provide most of our information regarding the religion of pre-conquest Canaan, previously known to us only from the Old Testament, from Phoenician and Punic texts and inscriptions, and from the account given by Philo of Byblos (about A.D. 100) of the work of Sanchuniaton (who probably lived before Trojan times), the author of a history of Phoenicia which Philo claimed to have translated.

From the Ras Shamra tablets we gather that among the chief deities were El, father of the gods; his wife Asherah; and their children Baal, god of rain and fertility, Anath his sister and lover, and Mot, sometimes representing death, sometimes summer heat, his enemy. There was a system of priesthood and of sacrifice, probably both animal and human, which took place not only in temples but also at open-air sanctuaries, the 'hill shrines' of the Old Testament. The whole religion was bound up with the vicissitudes of the seasons and the need to ensure fertility in crops and people. This, it was believed, came about by the union of the gods, which in turn was effected or at least stimulated by sexual intercourse between humans at the sanctuaries. The practice of religious prostitution resulted.

How much of all this did Israel assimilate? There are Old Testament references to child sacrifice, the use of hill shrines, and the worship of Baal and Asherah; indeed Manasseh, king of Judah between 687 and 642 B.C., managed to combine all these practices and is roundly condemned for it in 2 Kings 21: 1–9. The prophets passionately protested against religious prostitution (Jer. 2:

20, Hos. 4: 13, 14); obviously this idea like the others had gained a hold but was discouraged with vigour.

On the positive side, Hebrew poetry, behind which lies the established literary tradition of the ancient Near East, has particular affinity with Ugaritic poetry not only in parallelism and imagery but at times in thought. Like Baal, Yahweh rides above the earth (Ps. 68: 4), the lightning is his arrow, the thunder his voice (Ps. 18: 13, 14). The Baal myth reads

> Behold, thine enemies, O Baal,
> Behold, thine enemies thou shalt smite,
> Behold, thou shalt subdue thine adversaries,

whilst Ps. 92: 9 (N.E.B. alternative translation) has

> For behold thy foes, O LORD,
> thy foes will surely perish,
> all evildoers will be scattered.

Two legends of ancient kings, Keret, and Aqhat son of Dan'el (the same name is found in the Hebrew text of Ezek. 14: 14, 20), suggests that Israel's ideas of monarchy may owe something to Canaan. Yasib, son of Keret,

> sits in the palace
> And his inwards instruct him,
> Go to thy father, Yasib,
> Go to thy father, and say...
> 'Thou dost not judge the case of the widow,
> Nor decide the suit of the oppressed.'

In this Yasib shows himself a worthy forerunner of Absalom the son of David, who would say to would-be litigants, 'I can see that you have a very good case, but you will get no hearing from the king...If only I were appointed judge in the land, it would be my business to see that everyone who brought a suit or a claim got justice from me' (2 Sam. 15: 3, 4).

The Aqhat epic, too, defines part of the duty of a king as

> Deciding the case of the widow,
> Judging the suit of the orphan,

in agreement with Ps. 72, which prays

> That he may judge thy people rightly
> and deal out justice to the poor and suffering...
> May he have pity on the needy and the poor,
> deliver the poor from death (Ps. 72: 2, 13).

Seven fragmentary tablets recount two myths about Baal. In the first story Baal gains his kingship by defeating the tyrannical waters, elsewhere identified with the serpent Lotan (Leviathan), and, as we have already seen, this theme of conflict occurs in both the Babylonian epics and the Old Testament. It seems possible, too, that it helped to widen the Israelite concept of the power and influence of Yahweh, which may have been developed in an annual New Year Festival held at Jerusalem to celebrate his kingship.

The second myth has as its theme the tension between fertility, represented by Baal, and sterility, represented by Mot. Baal is slain by Mot, then vengeance is taken by Anath, Baal is revived, and plenty returns. Clearly this has some connection with the yearly cycle of drought, rain and growth, and the story may have been enacted annually (or, according to some evidence, every seven years), as part of the rite to encourage fertility. It is the local variation of the Tammuz, Osiris and Dionysus myths of Babylonia, Egypt and Greece, but has it any counterpart in Hebrew thought? Knowledge of it may possibly be indicated in Hos. 6: 1–3, which speaks of

God reviving his people and coming to their rescue 'like spring rains that water the earth', and the exultant lines after the triumph of Baal:

> The heavens rain oil
> The wadis run with honey

may find an echo in Ps. 65: 11:

> Thou dost crown the year with thy good gifts
> and the palm-trees drip with sweet juice,

and in Ps. 68: 9:

> Of thy bounty, O God, thou dost refresh with rain
> thy own land in its weariness.

But in the Old Testament there is no thought of a yearly dying and rising god whose well-being must be ensured before rain is given. Israel may have used some of the Canaanite imagery to convey the might and majesty of Yahweh, but the concepts of his changelessness and sovereign justice owe no more to Ugarit than to Mesopotamia.

Two accounts of a battle: the Moabite Stone

According to the Old Testament, relations between Israel and the land of Moab, to the east of the Dead Sea, were always uneasy. In the time of the judges Moab harassed Israel (Judg. 3: 12–30), then later she was subjugated and made tributary by David (2 Sam. 8: 2). Solomon took Moabite women into his harem and built a shrine to their god Kemosh (1 Kings 11: 7), but after his reign Moab must have regained her independence, for our next information is that she was conquered by Omri, king of Israel, in the latter part of the ninth century B.C.

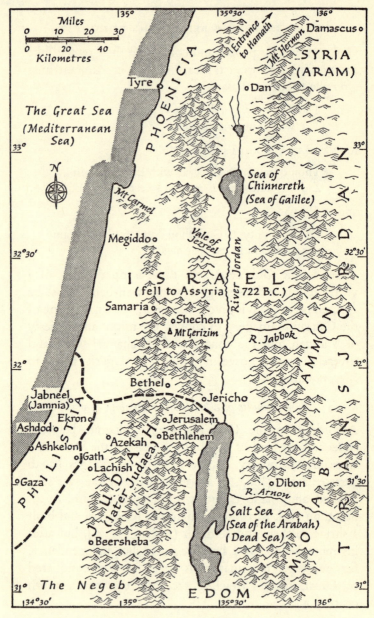

3. The Kingdoms of Israel and Judah from the death of Solomon to the Babylonian exile

This knowledge comes to us not from the Bible but from the Moabite Stone, a slab of black basalt first discovered at Dhibhan (ancient Dibon) in Transjordan in 1868, which after being broken up by local Arabs was eventually pieced together and placed in the Louvre. The thirty-four line inscription, dated about 830 B.C., tells rather boastfully how Mesha king of Moab with the help of Kemosh successfully rebelled against the house of Omri. 'Omri king of Israel', says Mesha, 'he oppressed Moab many days, for Kemosh was angry with his land. And his son succeeded him, and he too said, "I will oppress Moab." In my days he spake (thus), and I saw my desire upon him and upon his house, when Israel perished utterly for ever.' A detailed report of the campaign follows.

This account, taken side by side with the information given in 2 Kings 3, is important because of both the likenesses and the discrepancies between them. The language closely resembles biblical Hebrew in grammar, syntax and vocabulary, and several place names are mentioned which also appear in the Old Testament. There are religious similarities which emphasize the extent to which Israel was bound up with her neighbours. Kemosh is angry with his people, delivers them over to their enemies, and ultimately saves them – a pattern familiar to us from Judg. 2: 16–19 and elsewhere. He says, 'Go, take Nebo against Israel', just as Yahweh encourages David against the Philistines (1 Sam. 23: 4), and when the victory is won Mesha 'devotes' the city to his god by applying the same principle of total destruction as is enjoined in Josh. 6: 17.

As far as the actual events are concerned, the Moabite story supplements the Old Testament by explaining that it was Omri who had re-conquered Moab – a fact not mentioned in the unenthusiastic summary of that monarch's reign given in 1 Kings 16: 23–8. The accounts agree that during the time of Ahab the Moabites were subject to Israel, that there was a rebellion, and that it was successful. But there are a number of disagreements. The inscription places the rebellion half way through the reign of Ahab, Omri's son; the Bible states that it happened after Ahab's death (2 Kings 1: 1, 3: 5). In fact, the inscription is in itself inconsistent, for the 'forty years' of oppression which it mentions would end in the reign not of Ahab but of Jehoram, Ahab's son and Omri's grandson; we must either take 'forty years' as a conventional number or read 'grandson' for 'son' of Omri.

When we come to the battle, 2 Kings 3 claims that Jehoram with his allies almost crushed the revolt, and that Mesha only saved the day by publicly sacrificing his son to Kemosh and so demoralizing his enemies to the point of flight. Mesha himself, however, makes no mention of this incident, but gives a list of unhindered victories ending in the liquidation of Israel. We can only assume that this is a classic case of each side emphasizing its successes and playing down its setbacks, and we are reminded that both these accounts were written by partisan rather than detached observers.

The last years of Judah: some contemporary Judaean
correspondence. The Lachish letters

The events surrounding the first fall of Jerusalem in 597 B.C. are described in the Babylonian Chronicle from the conqueror's point of view; the Lachish letters give a glimpse of the following years, this time as seen by the conquered.

In 1935 J. L. Starkie, leader of the Wellcome Archaeological Research Expedition to the Near East, discovered
on the site of ancient Lachish, to the south-west of
Jerusalem, pottery fragments bearing pen-and-ink inscriptions in ancient Hebrew. These eighteen potsherds,
together with a further three found in 1938, yielded about
a hundred more or less readable lines of script, written in
the time of the prophet Jeremiah. Now scattered in
museums and libraries over the world (some in the
British Museum), they are all that is left of a series of
letters sent to one Yaosh, military commander of Lachish,
by his subordinate Hoshaiah, in charge of one of the out-
posts between the larger fortresses of Lachish and
Azekah. Their date is approximately 590–588 B.C., the
later years of Zedekiah, Nebuchadnezzar's vassal king.
Jer. 34: 7 records a time when 'the army of the king of
Babylon was attacking Jerusalem and the remaining
cities of Judah, namely Lachish and Azekah. These were
the only fortified cities left in Judah.'

As with any one-sided correspondence, it is none too
easy to reconstruct the specific circumstances, but in one
of the fragments (Letter III), Hoshaiah is apparently
justifying himself concerning some important documents which have passed through his hands. Perhaps he
was suspected of reading them when he should not, or
worse still of passing on their contents; at any rate he
indignantly denies any knowledge of them, and says, 'The
heart of thy servant hath been sick since thou didst
write unto thy servant.'

In Letter IV the problem is the breakdown of the system
of communications. The outpost is dependent on signals
from Lachish, for they 'cannot see Azekah' – whether
because of climatic conditions or a failure at Azekah is not

33

clear. Letter VI returns to the political situation. Correspondence has been forwarded from the king and princes of Judah, and Hoshaiah is critical of its tone. 'And behold', he writes, 'the words of the princes are not good, but to weaken our hands and to slacken the hands of the men who are informed about them.' During the final siege of Jerusalem Jeremiah himself was the target for a similar accusation: 'By talking in this way he is discouraging' (i.e. 'weakening the hands of') 'the soldiers and the rest of the people left in the city. He is pursuing not the people's welfare but their ruin' (Jer. 38: 4).

These letters are of linguistic value in that they show us exactly the kind of language and script which Judaeans were using at this period. They demonstrate, too, the formal style of letter writing; the complimentary opening, 'May Yahweh cause my lord to hear tidings of peace', or 'May Yahweh cause my lord to see this season in good health', and the self-deprecating reference to 'thy servant' are not forgotten even in an emergency.

More important, however, is the fact that they are among the very few surviving pieces of Hebrew writing which are contemporary with the events they describe. They evoke vividly the political intrigues and military hazards of the time, and the anxiety of the writer to justify himself to his superior. The numerous mentions of other commanders and messengers, and the cryptic references to problems and misunderstandings, all contribute to the atmosphere of tension. They supplement the records in the Old Testament, and counterbalance the detached indifference of the Babylonian history.

THE LITERATURE OF EGYPT

Egypt was the home of settled communities from about 5000 B.C., but her history proper is usually reckoned from 3100 B.C., the date of the first of her thirty dynasties. There were three periods of power and influence: the Old Kingdom from 2686 to 2160 B.C.; the Middle Kingdom from 2160 to 1786 B.C.; and the New Kingdom from 1568 to 1085 B.C., followed by a long gradual decline until 332 B.C. when Egypt was conquered by Alexander the Great. Apart from the changes in the royal house there is a certain stability in this long story in that subjugation by a foreign power, such as the Hyksos kings who ruled from 1750 B.C. until the beginning of the New Kingdom, was the exception rather than the rule.

In religion, too, although things changed and developed over the centuries, the people who could 'learn but never forget' seldom abandoned a belief, however primitive. As a result there were many gods, animate and inanimate, cosmic and even human, but the emphasis was on the religious system and its observances rather than on doctrine, and on the whole there was an absence of fanaticism and excess.

At the centre of life was the Pharaoh, the divine king identified with the god Horus, and the source of all activity whether religious, political, military or social. In the background was the Nile, enabling man to live surrounded by desert in the land which Hecataeus of Miletus called 'the gift of the river'. All in all it is not surprising that the Egyptian view of the world order was fairly stable. The perfection instituted when the first god-king brought kingship to the earth had been tarnished, so expectations for the future meant a nostalgic hope for the return of the Golden Age of the past rather than a restless pressing forward towards an ideal society in the future.

Geographically and politically, Egypt was to a certain extent isolated by the deserts to the west and east, but from the north and south she was vulnerable. She needed Syria–Palestine as a buffer state, and from 2000 B.C. secured footholds there and in Asia. The Tell el-Amarna letters record her involvement at the end of this long period of fluctuating power. Biblical references to Egypt, from Abram's sojourn to the Egyptian attempt to help Jerusalem in the last stand against Babylon (Gen. 12: 10–20, Jer. 37: 5), are frequent and mainly disapproving. By contrast, Egyptian records have comparatively little to say about Israel, but even so they have their own contribution to make to our understanding of the Old Testament.

Customs and names: the Execration Texts

In 1926 texts were published, taken from the inscriptions on fragments of pottery found at Thebes, dating from the eighteenth and nineteenth centuries B.C. Known as the Execration Texts, and now in the Berlin Museum, they are the outcome of the Egyptian custom of writing on bowls the names of actual or potential enemies to be cursed. It was believed that the breaking of the bowl brought the curse into effect by sympathetic magic. A variation of the practice was to write the names on clay figurines representing the enemy, which were either smashed or buried. Figurines carrying this kind of curse are in the Cairo and Brussels Museums.

Sometimes the enemies were described not by name but in general terms, according to a set formula, such as 'All men, all people, all males, all eunuchs, all women, and all officials, who may rebel, who may plot, who may fight...and every rebel who talks of rebelling – in this entire land.' Or the curse might be against more indefinite forces: 'Every evil word, every evil speech, every evil slander, every evil thought, every evil plot, every evil fight, every evil quarrel, every evil plan, every evil thing, all evil dreams and all evil slumber.'

The texts are of interest for the study of the Old Testament from several points of view. First, the destruction of enemies through a ritual act is not without analogy. In Jer. 19: 1–13 the prophet, at Yahweh's command, breaks an earthen jar with the words: 'These are the words of the LORD of Hosts: Thus will I shatter this people and this city as one shatters an earthen vessel so that it cannot be mended.' This is not of course to say that Jeremiah's symbolic action was the same as or even dependent on the execration rite, but the underlying ideas are not dissimilar.

Secondly, some of the place names in Syria–Palestine mentioned in the fragments, for example Ashkelon, Jerusalem, Shechem and Tyre, are also mentioned in the Bible. Apparently these cities had displeased Egypt by rebelling against her suzerainty, and so we get a glimpse of the extent of Egyptian power during the period of the patriarchal stories. The fact that the earlier Execration Texts refer to places on the coast, whilst the later ones also include parts of the upper Jordan valley, may indicate the way in which Egypt's dominions increased, but we cannot be too sure of this, since the names of the loyal princes and peoples are of course absent from texts cursing the disloyal.

Thirdly, the names of some of the rulers of these cities are interesting. Similar names are found in the Mari texts of the same period (see p. 9), and as they are Semitic rather than Akkadian in origin one deduces that they must have belonged to immigrants into Mesopotamia. The same formation is also found in some of the old Israelite names, and so it is not impossible that this is early evidence of the movements of population to which Israel in turn belonged.

The Jews under Persian rule in Egypt:
the Elephantine Papyri

Elephantine, an island on the Nile opposite Assuan, was the home of a Jewish military colony during the fifth century B.C. Papyri purchased in the late nineteenth and early twentieth centuries and published between 1906 and 1953 give us some idea of the life and history of this community. The papyri bear dates between 495 B.C. and the end of the fifth century B.C. and are written in Aramaic, the language of trade and diplomacy which was gradually to oust Hebrew as the everyday speech of the Jews. Some of the texts can be seen in the British Museum, others in the Brooklyn Museum; they include legal documents, letters, and religious texts. From them we gather that the colony was in existence before the Persians conquered Egypt in 525 B.C. and, though less certainly, that it disappeared sometime after the end of their domination in 404 B.C.

Religion at Elephantine centred round the temple of Yahweh, or Yahu. A temple subscription list shows gifts to Ishum-bethel and Anath-bethel as well as to Yahu, and in other texts Anath-Yahu and Herem-bethel are mentioned. These names suggest that other gods were worshipped alongside Yahu; Anath (the name of the ancient Canaanite goddess) may even have been his consort. But this is far from certain. The names can be translated 'Name of the house of God', 'Sign of Yahu (or of the house of God)', and 'Sacredness of the house of God', and may only have been titles describing different aspects of Yahu.

Of the letters, the most important is the one, known from two surviving rough drafts, addressed in 407 B.C. by the Jewish leaders of the colony to Bagoas, the Persian governor of Judaea. The temple of Yahu had been destroyed by the Egyptians in 410 B.C., and help in rebuilding is requested. A memorandum embodying Bagoas' verbal reply agrees that 'it be rebuilt in its place as it was before, and that meal-offering and incense be offered upon that altar, as was formerly done'. Animal sacrifice is not mentioned, and further correspondence concerning the proposed new temple confirms that it was not sanctioned, whether in deference to the religious susceptibilities of the Egyptians or of the Persians we cannot tell.

The Elephantine documents are connected in various ways with the Old Testament. The letter to Bagoas, and the so-called 'Passover papyrus', an order by Darius II that the Feast of Unleavened Bread must be celebrated by the colony, confirm the impression given in the book of Ezra that the Persian kings took an interest in Jewish religious matters. The letter also mentions 'Delaiah and Shelemiah, the sons of Sanballat the governor of Samaria' and 'the High priest Johanan and his colleagues the priests in Jerusalem'. By this time the said Sanballat is apparently an elderly man, but in his heyday he was Nehemiah's leading opponent (Neh. 2: 19, etc.), whilst Johanan was a contemporary of Ezra (Ezra 10: 6) and the grandson of Eliashib, high priest in Nehemiah's time (Neh. 12: 23). These references from Elephantine help in sorting out the difficulty of the respective dates of Nehemiah and Ezra, by indicating that Nehemiah's work must have been earlier in the fifth century than the letter to Bagoas, and that he probably preceded Ezra in Jerusalem. Thus the 'twentieth year of King Artaxerxes' (Neh. 2: 1), when he asked permission to return to Judaea, will have been 445 B.C., in the reign of Artaxerxes I.

Perhaps most interesting, however, is the picture which we are given of a well-organized, religious but highly distinctive community of Jews living in biblical times yet not mentioned in the Bible. At the very time when, according to Ezra–Nehemiah, attempts were being made in Jerusalem to enforce the exclusiveness of Jewish religion, the leaders at Elephantine, either ignorant of or ignoring the Deuteronomic law that all sacrifice was to be offered at the Jerusalem temple, were asking for help in rebuilding their own sanctuary. We can only guess that the temple of Yahu must have been built before the law of the central sanctuary was fully implemented, and that the colony clung to its local cult on account of conviction, or convenience, or both.

The wisdom of Egypt and Israel: the Teaching of Amen-em-opet

'Wisdom' in ancient Israel was the ability to cope with life. It could be manifested in many ways: good craftsmanship (Exod. 28: 3), good administration (Deut. 1: 13), intellectual brilliance (1 Kings 4: 29 ff.), or shrewd commonsense (1 Kings 3: 16–28), but always it involved the capacity to assess a situation and act for the best. In course of time, therefore, it came to be linked with ethical judgements, explicitly or implicitly related to the will of God.

Under the monarchy, 'the Wise' may have been a distinct class, like priests and prophets; Jer. 18: 18 speaks of 'priests to guide us...wise men to advise...prophets to proclaim the word'. One of the tasks of these 'wise men' was to advise on royal policy, and that despite the belief that special wisdom was invested in the king. For instance, in 2 Sam. 14: 20 the wise woman of Tekoa says to David, 'Your majesty is as wise as the angel of God', but none the less she influences his decision regarding Absalom. After the exile the wise men still gave counsel and instruction, by this time to anyone who would 'lodge in their house of learning' (Ecclus. 51: 23), and collections of their sayings are preserved in the 'wisdom books', among them Job, Proverbs, Ecclesiastes, Ecclesiasticus, the Wisdom of Solomon, Tobit, and 4 Maccabees. This literature usually takes the form either of short proverbial sayings or of longer reflections upon the meaning of life. Sometimes wisdom is personified – as the Law, providing the framework for a well-orientated way of life, or as a divine agency at work in creation (Ecclus. 24: 1–23, Prov. 8: 22–30).

Wisdom and the wise also appear in the literatures of Sumer, Babylon and Ugarit, but it is in Egyptian writings that they are most prominent. As early as 2450 B.C. Ptah-hotep, chief counsellor to the Pharaoh, wrote down for his son what he had learnt from a lifetime's experience, 'For', he says, 'there is no-one born wise'. In the subsequent long tradition of wisdom in Egypt there are many affinities with the Old Testament, but the most remarkable occur in a work called 'The Teaching of Amen-em-opet'. This papyrus, believed to have come from Thebes, is now in the British Museum; suggested dates for the work vary from 1300 to 600 B.C.

The author's message, addressed like that of Ptah-hotep to his son, is less materialistic and more spiritual than that of his predecessors. The source of true morality is religion, and he who lives in obedience to this principle will have worldly success as well as moral well-being. The ideal man is tranquil and silent,

> He is like a tree growing in a garden...
> Its fruit is sweet, its shade is pleasant,

whilst his opposite, the hot-head, is

> Like a tree growing in the open,
> In the completion of a moment (comes) its loss of foliage.

This simile is found in Ps. 1:3, which describes the godly man as

> like a tree
> planted beside a watercourse,

and in Jer. 17:6, where by contrast the ungodly is

> like a juniper in the desert;
> when good comes he shall not see it.

Elsewhere, Amen-em-opet shows affinities with the historical books (1 Sam. 2:6 ff.) and with the Code of Holiness (Lev. 19:14). But the most striking parallels are with the book of Proverbs, especially chapters 22:17-24: 22. Advice from Amen-em-opet on going out to dinner is

> Do not eat bread before a noble,
> Nor lay on thy mouth at first...
> Look at the cup which is before thee
> And let it serve thy needs,

whilst Prov. 23:1-3 has

> When you sit down to eat with a ruling prince,
> be sure to keep your mind on what is before you...
> Do not be greedy for his dainties,
> for they are not what they seem.

On friendship, Amen-em-opet says:

> Do not associate to thyself the heated man
> Nor visit him for conversation,

and Prov. 22: 24 counsels

> Never make friends with an angry man
> nor keep company with a bad-tempered one.

Many passages are so close in language as well as in meaning that the Egyptian work has helped to solve some of the textual difficulties in Proverbs. For instance Prov. 22: 20, 'Here I have written out for you thirty sayings', made doubtful sense until it was realized that the Teaching of Amen-em-opet is arranged in thirty chapters, and that the compiler of this section of Proverbs adopted the same principle as a basis for his collection of thirty maxims of roughly four verses each.

The similarities between the two works are too close to be coincidental, but what is the actual relationship? Suggestions are that the writer of Proverbs used Amen-em-opet, perhaps in an Aramaic translation; or that both authors borrowed from an earlier original; or that the proverbial literature of the Near East was international, and was assimilated by Israel just as readily as by her neighbours.

It certainly seems that ancient wisdom knew no national boundaries, and that superficially there is little to choose between Hebrew and other varieties. There are few references to Israelite religious institutions in the Old Testament wisdom literature, and the name of God, which occurs infrequently, might almost be exchanged for that of Re or Horus without too much alteration in sense. But these impressions are misleading. It is the fear of Yahweh which is the beginning of wisdom, and this quality creates a faith and a whole way of life which the invocation of Re or Horus could not produce. Yet again Israel has used the ideas and assimilated the thought forms of her environment without relinquishing her distinctive religious ideals.

CONCLUSION

What does all this amount to? Obviously the records of Israel's neighbours are important for Old Testament studies, but it is possible to exaggerate this importance. In the first place, although these documents are older than any Old Testament manuscripts which we possess, their antiquity does not automatically guarantee complete accuracy. Mistakes could occur in 2000 B.C. just as easily as in later centuries. Secondly, archaeological evidence must not be confused with historical proof. Extra-biblical sources can confirm, elucidate, supplement, counterbalance or conflict with biblical accounts, but it is asking too much if we expect them to provide infallible proof or disproof of the historicity of actual persons or events. Thirdly, as we have already seen, similarities in religious literature do not necessarily imply that there was compatibility in outlook and basic belief. Fourthly, it must be remembered that a word which is ostensibly the same in two languages may in fact bear two completely different meanings. For instance, in Egypt the Pharaoh was obliged to maintain *maat*, or right order – a concept apparently similar to the *tsedeq*, or righteousness, asked for the Israelite king in Ps. 72: 1. Yet *maat* to the Egyptians was personified by the goddess Re, and inseparable from the Pharaoh's divine status, whilst in Israel *tsedeq*, though an attribute of Yahweh, could only come *from* him and be bestowed *by* him on the king.

Perhaps, however, it is most important of all to bear in mind the problems of interpretation which arise when we compare living and dead traditions. The Near Eastern texts, of which we have examined only a small proportion, record beliefs and ways of life which disappeared thousands of years ago; attempts to revive these religions or to study their documents as living literature would be useless if not impossible. The Old Testament likewise records the historical and religious progress of an ancient nation, but it also does much more. Far from being buried and then excavated centuries later, it has provided a continuing tradition and a source of constant study; people have read it, re-examined it and lived by it. If we write it off as an interesting account of matters too far away to have any relevance to the twentieth century we shall fail to reckon with its integral place in contemporary religious thought, as well as with the light which it sheds on the New Testament.

SUGGESTIONS FOR FURTHER READING

G. R. DRIVER and J. C. MILES *The Babylonian Laws*, Oxford, 1952 & 1955.

J. FINEGAN *Light from the Ancient Past*, London, 1946.

H. G. MAY *Oxford Bible Atlas*, London, 1962.

S. MOSCATI *The Face of the Ancient Orient*, London, 1960.

J. B. PRITCHARD *Ancient Near Eastern Texts relating to the Old Testament*, Princeton, 1950 (3rd edition, 1970).

——*Archaeology and the Old Testament*, Princeton and London, 1958.

D. WINTON THOMAS (ed.) *Documents from Old Testament Times*, London, 1958.

G. E. WRIGHT *Biblical Archaeology*, London and Philadelphia, 1957.

2

THE POETRY AND PROSE OF
THE OLD TESTAMENT

A VARIETY OF LITERATURE

The Old Testament and Apocrypha contain writings
from different periods and of varying types, lengths and
subjects. Here are a few examples.

Myth

This is often popularly understood as a purely fictitious
story, or as the product of an over-active imagination. A
reference to someone's 'mythical fortune' usually implies that we do not believe in its existence. Yet in the
religious sense 'myth' has a very different meaning and a
much deeper purpose. It presents in pictorial language
ideas about the world and about God (or the gods).
Ritual (the acts performed during religious ceremonies)
seeks to do the same thing by action and visual representation. It may be, though we cannot be sure about this, that
for thousands of years myth and ritual have been closely
related. One theory is that in primitive religions myth
was the spoken word which accompanied certain ritual
actions and, it was thought, helped to make them valid. It
described what was happening, but at the same time saw
in it a deeper significance. For instance, as we have seen,
ancient Canaan, like Babylonia, preserved the story of a
primaeval combat between the gods and chaos or death,
and at one time this was probably re-enacted annually,
or perhaps every seven years, thus ensuring fertility
during the coming yearly or seven-yearly cycle. The

accompanying words, or 'myth', described these actions, but also saw them as a representation of the events of Creation. When the ritual was no longer performed, the myth often survived (as was the case with the Canaanite Baal myths and the Babylonian myth of Creation), and of course its value then lay in the lasting ideas which it embodied.

There is no definite proof that this kind of enactment took place in Israelite religion, but, as we have seen (p. 6), there are references in the Old Testament to a conflict between Yahweh and the monsters of chaos. These, together with some of the Genesis stories such as the Creation and Flood narratives, bear enough resemblance to the mythology of other religions to justify their inclusion in the category of myth in its deepest and most lasting sense. But in their portrayal of the great themes of creation, sin, judgement and forgiveness, they owe little to other cultures; they reflect Israel's own religious beliefs.

Saga and legend

These are names given to types of story related to and yet distinct from myth. *Saga* deals with places or people of some significance or importance. The story of Sodom in Gen. 19 explains the unfruitfulness of that particular area; Gen. 25: 21–6 relates the birth of Esau and Jacob to the future of their tribes; other sagas, often extended in length, of leaders and heroes include those of Moses, the judges, Saul, Jonathan and David. This form of narrative is later revived in 1 Macc. 6: 42–7, which tells of the self-sacrifice of Eleazar Avaran.

In referring to biblical stories where the places, people or events concerned have a specifically religious significance, perhaps because they are sanctuaries, or priests, or prophets, or festivals, the narrative is called *legend*. This also is often misunderstood; when used of biblical material it means an episode which may be based on historical fact and which gives an explanation which is religious, yet without the depth and eternal significance of myth. For instance, legend might be used to explain a place name such as Beer-lahai-roi, 'the Well of the Living One of Vision' (Gen. 16: 7–14), or a custom such as a food taboo (Gen. 32: 32 ends the story of Jacob wrestling with the stranger with 'This is why the Israelites to this day do not eat the sinew of the nerve that runs in the hollow of the thigh; for the man had struck Jacob on that nerve in the hollow of the thigh'). Or, by its recital of the life and deeds of a particular character, legend might make some spiritual or devotional point, as in the stories of the stand made by Daniel and his companions against Babylonian religious pressure (Dan. 1–6).

Historical narrative

Does the Old Testament contain any straightforward reporting of actual events? There are the 'annals', or records of official archivists, which are incorporated in Kings and Chronicles and have their parallels in other Near Eastern literature. There is autobiography, often describing visionary experience, as in Isa. 6 and Zech. 1–8; and there are books such as Ruth and Esther, written in something of the style of the historical novel. But none of this is quite the same as a contemporary, factual chronicle. The account of the reigns of the first three kings of Israel (1 Sam. 8 to 1 Kings 11) has perhaps a strong claim to be described in this way. Yet when we examine these passages in detail, they are by no means consistent or simple. There are two accounts of the first meeting of Saul and

David and two accounts of the rejection of Saul; two different attitudes to the monarchy are described; David twice spares Saul's life; and the last four chapters of 2 Samuel have the appearance of an appendix. The central part of the section, 2 Sam. 9–20 and 1 Kings 1 and 2, is known as the 'Court History' or 'Succession Narrative', because it deals with the struggle for the succession to David's throne. Again, however, a closer scrutiny reveals the possibility that this account may be made up of political propaganda justifying Solomon's succession, plus moral and religious precepts exemplified in the lives of its chief characters, as well as of factual information. Or it may be even more theological in intent – the work of later priestly writers who, themselves involved in the worship of the Jerusalem sanctuary, were trying to deal with the question, 'Why was it Solomon who built the temple?' It seems that Old Testament history, like all history, repays study by showing its true complexity.

Legal material

In particular the first five books of the Old Testament (the Pentateuch, see p. 14) contain a great deal of law, dealing with life's religious, civil, social, economic and personal aspects. It is presented in longer collections, such as the Book of the Covenant (Exod. 20: 22 – 23: 33) and the Holiness Code (Lev. 17–26), and shorter ones like the two forms of the Ten Commandments in Exod. 20: 3–17 and Deut. 5: 7–21. The longer collections themselves incorporate smaller ones; Exod. 21: 1 – 22: 16, designated 'laws', is part of the Book of the Covenant, and Lev. 21 and 22, giving particular requirements for priests and sacrifices, is included in the Holiness Code but was probably originally independent. There has been so much editing at different times, with consequent over-lapping and repetition, that one can hardly hope to make a complete analysis of Old Testament law along these lines. All the same, it is a help to remember this long process when we study the legal requirements of the Pentateuch. If we are to understand them, we must try to find out what we can first about the situations in which the laws were originally framed, and then about the changes which later necessitated reiteration or revision.

Prophetic oracle

Although prophecy in Israel existed as early as the time of Samuel (1 Sam. 3:20, 9:9, 10:5) or even Moses (Deut. 34: 10), and much information about prophets such as Nathan, Elijah and Elisha is included in the books of Samuel and Kings, the main body of Old Testament prophetic literature is to be found in the four collections of prophecy known as Isaiah, Jeremiah, Ezekiel and 'the Twelve'. (These last are the so-called minor prophets, beginning with Hosea and ending with Malachi.)

These books, sometimes called the writing prophets, or, in the Hebrew Old Testament, the Latter Prophets (see p. 113), make use of many literary forms, among them autobiography, sermon, record, prayer, and poetry ranging from funeral dirge (Amos 5: 2) to drinking song (Isa. 22: 13), but they also contribute their own distinctive form, the prophetic oracle. Usually poetic in style, this may begin 'These are the words of the Lord' (Isa. 10: 24), a formula of the type used by messengers throughout the ancient Near East, or it may have 'This is the very word of the LORD' (Amos 3: 15) at the end or in the middle. It thus claims to be a direct proclamation of Yahweh's will, with people and events seen in the light of the prophet's understanding of the nature of God. It is therefore concerned with its contemporary situation; Amos 5: 21–4:

> I hate, I spurn your pilgrim-feasts...
> Let justice roll on like a river
> and righteousness like an ever-flowing stream,

and also with the future which may arise from that situation; warnings and promises concerning the consequences of obedience and disobedience may be given; Isa. 1: 19, 20:

> Obey with a will,
> and you shall eat the best that earth yields;
> but, if you refuse and rebel,
> locust-beans shall be your only food.

Or it may look to the ultimate triumph of God's will in the coming Golden Age; Mic. 4: 1–4:

> In days to come...
> nation shall not lift sword against nation
> nor ever again be trained for war,
> and each man shall dwell under his own vine,
> under his own fig-tree, undisturbed

(see also Isa. 2: 2–4). Opinions differ as to whether these oracles were originally spoken as we now have them, or whether they are collections of shorter sayings spoken at different times.

Wisdom and apocalyptic

As we have seen (p. 41), several of the later books of the Old Testament and of the Apocrypha reflect the kind of thinking on the meaning of life which was known in Israel and the Near East as *wisdom*. Another type of writing which is found not only in the Old Testament and Apocrypha but also predominantly in the literature between the Testaments is *apocalyptic*, owing its name to the Greek verb *apocalypto*, meaning 'I reveal' or 'I unveil'. It has been described as 'the child of prophecy', and may have had its roots in the prophetic passages dealing with the anticipated Golden Age which was yet to come. In the last centuries before Christ, this rather remote hope changed to a belief that the climax of history was imminent, and would come not by natural evolution but through the direct intervention of God. This outlook also owed something to the Jewish idea that God had intervened at such decisive moments in Israel's history as the exodus, though in the historical view he was in control of events but not acting alone in them, whilst apocalyptic thinking saw him as the sole intervener.

Apocalyptic does not claim the direct inspiration, authority and verbal expression of prophecy; the authors are writers rather than speakers. It usually takes an autobiographical form, and is either anonymous or written under an assumed name – often that of some hero of Israel's past. It is marked by a lavish use of symbolism (especially animal figures), by a view of history which divides it into sharply-defined ages, and by an almost exclusive concern with eschatology, that is, the 'last things' – the events of the end, which the writers believed to be at hand.

The Old Testament work with most apocalyptic characteristics is the book of Daniel, especially chapters 7 to 14, which record visions set in the sixth century B.C. but concerned with what was to come, culminating in the second-century reign of Antiochus Epiphanes, the tyrant whose religious oppression was the direct cause of the Maccabaean rebellion. (Some of these chapters have something in common with the type of prophecy, or 'pseudo-prophecy', practised by the Babylonians, who gave descriptions of the reigns of nameless kings in the form of predictions of the future.) Earlier Old Testament passages, such as Isa. 24–27, Ezek. 40–8, and Zech. 12–14, show some of the same features, and may indicate the transition from prophetic to apocalyptic writing. In the Apocrypha, 2 Esdras and Baruch belong to this type of literature, and there are fragments of a number of apocalypses among the Dead Sea Scrolls, as well as works such as the Enoch literature and the Assumption of Moses (see chapter 3).

HEBREW POETRY

Some of the forms of literature described above are prose, some are poetry, others, like the Creation Story in Genesis 1, are a sort of rhythmic prose which is somewhere between the two. But Hebrew poetry really merits a section to itself; not only because it has so many special characteristics but also because one-third of the Old Testament is poetry. In the Authorized Version this is not made clear, since poetry and prose are printed in much the same way, but in the more modern translations poems are set out as such, and we see that not only Psalms, Proverbs, the Song of Songs and Lamentations, but also many of the prophetic books, in part or in whole, are poetic in form. Even in the prose books there are snatches of poetry, like the Song of the Well in Num. 21: 17, 18:

> Well up, spring water! Greet it with song,
> the spring unearthed by the princes,
> laid open by the leaders of the people
> with sceptre and with mace,
> a gift from the wilderness.

Possibly some of these songs were originally incorporated in anthologies like the Book of Jashar (2 Sam. 1: 18) and the Book of the Wars of the LORD (Num. 21: 14), mentioned in the Old Testament but long since lost.

In the Apocrypha Ecclesiasticus, the Song of the Three and the Prayer of Manasseh are poetry, whilst Tobit, Judith and 1 Maccabees, though mainly prose, include shorter or longer poems, such as Judith's 'hymn of praise and thanksgiving' beginning

> Strike up a song to my God with tambourines;
> sing to the Lord with cymbals,

after the murder of Holophernes and the flight of the Assyrians (Judith 16: 2).

When we look at an English translation the basic features of Hebrew poetry are not immediately apparent:

> The earth is the LORD's and all that is in it,
> the world and those who dwell therein (Ps. 24: 1),

be it written as one line or as two, does not tell us whether in the original it rhymes or scans, or how the words are accented. In fact there is in Hebrew no rhyme or strict metre, but instead a correspondence (or sometimes a contrast) of ideas between lines or half-lines. This important principle was first clearly recognized as late as 1753 by Bishop Richard Lowth in his 'Lectures on the Sacred Poetry of the Hebrews', and was named by him '*parallelismus membrorum*' (parallelism of members).

Parallelism, as it is usually called, can be *synonymous*, where the thought is repeated, as in

So when judgement comes the wicked shall not stand firm, nor shall sinners stand in the assembly of the righteous
(Ps. 1: 5)

or *antithetic*, where there is a contrast between the two parts of a verse:

> The LORD watches over the way of the righteous,
> but the way of the wicked is doomed (Ps. 1: 6);

or, less obviously, *synthetic* or *formal*, where part two completes the sense of part one:

> When I was still young, before I set out on my travels,
> I asked openly for wisdom in my prayers (Ecclus. 51: 13).

Besides these three types distinguished by Bishop Lowth, there are other varieties, which might almost be described as variations on the fundamental patterns. *Emblematic* parallelism is synonymous in repeating its thought, but in one part of the line or couplet it uses simile or metaphor:

> As a father has compassion on his children,
> so has the LORD compassion on all who fear him
> (Ps. 103: 13).

In *stairlike* parallelism the thought 'climbs' by half-lines; part of line one is repeated as the starting-point for the idea in line two:

> I lift up my eyes to the hills,
> where shall *I find help*?
> *Help comes* only from the LORD,
> maker of heaven and earth (Ps. 121: 1, 2).

Inverted or *chiastic* parallelism reverses words or phrases, making a pattern which can be expressed as a–b–b–a. It derives from the Greek letter χ (chi): thus $_b^a\chi_a^b$:

> *a* We have escaped like a bird
> *b* from the fowler's trap;
> *b* the trap broke,
> *a* and so we escaped (Ps. 124: 7).

Apart from parallelism with all its variations, is there form or rhythm in Hebrew poetry? The most usual unit is the couplet (or *distich*, or *bicolon*), with its two lines (or *stichoi*, or *cola*); as in English poetry, several couplets are grouped together to make a stanza (or *strophe*). It is not always easy to see where a stanza ends, unless there is a refrain, such as

Let them thank the LORD for his enduring love
and for the marvellous things he has done for men
(Ps. 107: 8, 15, 21, 31),

or unless the poem is an acrostic, like Ps. 119, in which the initial letters of the stanzas spell out the Hebrew alphabet.

Rhythm has to be inferred from the parallelism itself, and from the traditional system of accentuated syllables evolved by the Massoretes (Hebrew = 'traditionalists'), the Jewish scholars who during the first nine centuries of the Christian era were concerned with the accurate transmission of the Hebrew text of the Old Testament. According to the Massoretes each word of more than one syllable receives one stress, usually on its last syllable, and a measure (that is, a line or half line) may contain three, four, five or even six stresses. But the measures in a poem need not all be of the same length; the metre of the *qinah*, or lament, is usually made up of alternate measures of three and two stresses; as one would expect, it is dominant in the book of Lamentations.

Other devices such as alliteration, onomatopoeia, play on words and assonance are used, although of course they are not obvious in translation. One of the most famous *word-plays* is that in Amos 8: 2, where the 'basket of ripe summer fruit' (*qais*, meaning 'summer'), in the prophet's vision, represents *qes*, the 'end' which threatens Israel. *Assonance* is the repetition of a vowel sound in the accentuated syllables of a sentence, for example, 'the *rain* in *Spain* falls *main*ly on the *plain*'. Ezek. 27: 27 exults over the downfall of Tyre, Israel's northern neighbour, comparing her with a gaily-bedecked merchant ship which sinks in mid-voyage:

> Your wealth, your staple wares, your imports,
> your sailors and your helmsmen,
> your caulkers, your merchants, and your warriors,
> all your ship's company,
> all who were with you.

In the Hebrew the long ē sound (as in 'day') occurs twelve times on the stressed syllables of this verse; the effect is one of disdain and contempt.

It would, however, be a barren kind of poetry which depended solely on literary form and mechanism; what of the meaning of the poems of the Old Testament, and the language in which it is expressed? There are poems for every day – love songs, work songs, drinking songs; poems for special occasions – weddings (Ps. 45), funerals (David's lament for Saul and Jonathan in 2 Sam. 1: 19–27), and victories (Moses' song of triumph in Exod. 15: 1–18). There are poems about wisdom, poems in the form of the prophetic oracle with its urgent message for the moment of crisis, and the sacred songs used in worship, of which the Psalms form the main collection. The language varies from simple to sophisticated; the style and form in which the poetry is written were, as we shall see, often dictated by what was accepted as correct for the particular occasion which inspired the writing.

But always the sentiments are vividly expressed, from the serenity and confidence of

The LORD is my shepherd;
I shall want nothing (Ps. 23: 1)

to the triumph, bordering on vindictiveness, of

So perish all thine enemies, O LORD;
but let all who love thee be like the sun rising in strength
(Judg. 5: 31).

Hebrew poetry takes us into the centre of the lives and thought of the authors and of the people on whose behalf they wrote. We are the richer that so much of it has survived.

THE STUDY OF OLD TESTAMENT LITERATURE

Here is this mass of literature: prose and poetry, law and prophecy, wisdom and apocalyptic, history, myth, legend and much else besides. The task of making sense of it all is daunting, but fortunately we are not the first to put our minds to this problem. For many years scholars have been looking at different parts of the Bible and asking, 'Who wrote this? and when? Where did his material come from, and why did he think it worth recording? What was – and is – the point of it all?' The last century or more has seen these questions and many others being put with increasing insistence, and as a result certain techniques have been worked out which we can apply to the book or books under investigation. These techniques are of course only tools, to be used selectively according to the particular problems which we are considering; nor is there any rigid order in which they must be applied. Sometimes the word 'criticism' is used, and this must be understood in a technical sense. It does not, as often in everyday speech, mean disparagement, or a negative attitude, or a lack of appreciation or respect, but rather the exercise of our powers of discernment in trying to study the Bible with honesty and integrity. The word itself is derived from the Greek *krino*, 'I judge', or 'I decide', which gives the key to its true meaning.

Textual criticism

(Sometimes called 'lower criticism'; 'higher criticism', or literary and historical analysis, is so called because it is nearer to the 'source'.)

This is often the first stage in serious study of the Bible, in that it tries to decide just what is to be studied. We have no original Old Testament manuscripts; the oldest which survive are copies, made hundreds of years after the books themselves were written, and in spite of the reputation for accuracy which the Hebrew scribes enjoyed, there are inevitably variations from time to time between these copies. A word, or a sentence, or even a single letter, may be included in one and omitted in another, or the order of words may vary, or there may even be a completely different piece of vocabulary in one or more manuscripts. The task of the textual critic is to compare readings which disagree and to decide which of them most probably represents the original.

In doing this he looks not only at the Hebrew manuscripts, but also at the ancient translations of the Old Testament into Greek, Aramaic and other languages. Ideally he is competent not only in Hebrew and in the languages of the Versions, as the ancient translations are called, but also in the 'cognate' languages, that is, all those which belong to the same family as Hebrew.

Whether these latter are 'dead' like Ugaritic, or 'living' like Arabic, the meaning of a word or phrase in their vocabularies may throw light on the correct form of a puzzling word in a biblical text, and may also help towards our understanding of it.

This study of manuscripts is inevitably bound up with matters of interpretation. How did a certain variant come about? Did it reflect the way in which the particular Jewish or Christian copyist understood the text, and was it therefore deliberate? Or even if it was almost certainly a careless mistake, could the very fact that the scribe made such an error be the result of the climate of thought in his day? It is rather as though a contemporary typist's mis-spelling of 'beetle' as 'beatle' were noticed in a manuscript discovered some hundreds of years hence. The context of the word would probably indicate that in this case it was meant to describe an insect rather than a pop singer; whilst a knowledge of the popular scene of the nineteen-sixties and seventies would help in dating the manuscript and accounting for the error.

We shall return to the subject of textual criticism in chapter 5, but perhaps enough has been said to make it clear that what may at first sight seem a purely technical and even rather arid kind of research cannot in fact be separated from some consideration of the ideas behind the text which we are studying.

Literary and historical analysis

Often referred to as 'source criticism' or 'higher criticism', this was the great preoccupation of scholars in the nineteenth and early twentieth centuries. Once the most likely text of a book has been established by means of the techniques of textual criticism, we can begin to read it and to recognize the different types of literature which it may include.

But we also notice some features which seem to require explanation. For instance, in Gen. 1: 1 to 2: 4*a* and 2: 4*b*–25 we find the creation of the world described twice, with considerable differences between the accounts. The first begins with a watery chaos and divides the work of creation into six separate operations culminating in the creation of animals and of mankind, male and female together. The second begins with a waterless waste but places the creation of man (male as distinct from female) first, and describes in some detail how he became a 'living creature' with the capacity for relationships with others. Or material may seem to have been re-written, expanded and reinterpreted in a second version, as in the account of the reign of king Ahaz of Judah in 2 Chron. 28, which is based on, yet very different from, the earlier story in 2 Kings 16; or it may be treated consecutively in one place and fragmentarily in another, like the items in Judg. 1, which are also to be found scattered throughout the latter part of the book of Joshua. Sometimes there is a change of atmosphere and attitude at a certain point in a book, as when the background of eighth-century Jerusalem in the first part of Isaiah changes at chapter 40 to that of Babylon in the sixth century B.C. Or there may be an alternation of two or more styles of writing, as in the Pentateuch, where God is sometimes called Yahweh, sometimes Elohim, and where in the Flood story it is even possible to unravel the two strands of narrative which have been woven into one.

All this raises problems. Are any of the Old Testament books the work of a single author, or are at any rate some of them composite, their final editors having drawn material from earlier sources and combined it into the finished product as we know it? And why, even allowing for differences in detail and emphasis, have certain stories been told twice, whilst others are to be found only once – and still others, presumably, not at all? Asking these and similar questions about the Pentateuch has led to the generally, though not universally, accepted view that it is a compilation and combination of four main sources (known by the letters J, E, D and P, and still sometimes thought of as actual documents, hence the name 'documentary theory') which were edited into their present form some time after the return of the Jews from their Babylonian exile of the sixth century B.C.

At times, too, an editor may have added to his earlier material; for instance some of the books of prophecy may consist of oracles recorded at or soon after the time of speaking, then afterwards not only edited but also augmented to present an up-to-date version of the prophet's known views and ideals (see p. 115). Indeed, Isa. 8: 16:

> Fasten up the message,
> seal the oracle with my teaching

(the N.E.B. footnote has the alternative 'among my disciples') is often interpreted as evidence of a circle of disciples who were entrusted with the task of preserving and communicating their master's teaching.

Investigation of the sources of a book leads to questions about date and authorship. When was it finally put together? Who was the author or editor? Why did he – or they – undertake the task? And how accurate is his record? It is here that we look at both *internal* and *external* evidence. *Internal* evidence is found within the text itself: evidence of the author's opinions, his style and vocabulary, the times in which he lived, the declared or implicit purpose of his work, the comparison of this particular book with any others attributed to his hand. The internal evidence of the Pentateuch indicates that its final editor is unlikely to have been Moses; that of Isaiah, that its prophecies probably represent the work of two or more people, over several centuries. *External* evidence is of course outside the Bible. It includes the evidence of literature from related cultures, such as the Babylonian Creation and Flood stories or the ancient Near Eastern law codes, which may have a bearing on the biblical text; contemporary or near-contemporary inscriptions like the Moabite Stone or the Lachish letters (pp. 29–34); and tradition and opinion on the material in question as far back as they are recorded.

It seems strange to us that this kind of analysis was not systematically applied to the Bible until comparatively recently. In fact, from early Christian times there were sporadic investigations like that of Theodore of Mopsuestia (about A.D. 350–428) into the authorship of Job (which he concluded was non-Jewish), but these touched only on isolated questions which took the investigator's fancy. Nor did the Reformation on the whole introduce this type of criticism, though the doubts expressed by Luther and Calvin on whether certain books (Hebrews, James, Jude and Revelation) really belonged to the Bible at all foreshadowed it. However, in the seventeenth and eighteenth centuries a spirit of enquiry and research developed in many disciplines. As a result of the Renaissance, the traditional view of the physical world (which was consistent with the biblical imagery of an earth held up by pillars, with the sky stretched above it) had been challenged by geographers and scientists; in addition, ancient documents in numerous disciplines were being investigated in a new and rigorous way with regard to composition and authorship. It is not therefore surprising that the pioneers who brought such ideas and techniques to bear on the Bible were not in the main theologians, but philosophers such as Hobbes and Spinoza and professional men such as Grotius the jurist and Astruc the medical professor. Even when literary and historical analysis had finally made its claim to be a theological discipline, the battle for its acceptance as such was still to come.

In the nineteenth century, insistence on inquiry without any presuppositions continued and deepened; one of the results was the documentary theory of the Pentateuch (see above), setting aside the traditional view of Moses as the author. In addition, contemporary ideas regarding evolution had their effect on biblical studies. A theory (now no longer universally popular) was worked out which traced the progress of Old Testament religion from primitive beginnings with the Patriarchs to Moses' introduction of Yahweh as the chief of the gods, then on through the struggles of the prophets to maintain Yahweh's supremacy, to the climax of the clearly-stated monotheism (belief in one true God alone) of the Babylonian exile:

> I am the LORD, there is no other;
> there is no god beside me (Isa. 45: 5).

The furore caused by such ideas can only be understood if we try to imagine their novel, disturbing and even in some cases apparently sacrilegious nature after centuries of comparatively unquestioning acceptance of traditional views about the Bible. Today we can examine these once-revolutionary theories objectively, knowing that some of them in their original forms were excessive or incomplete, and that some of the questions which they sought to answer have been superseded. Over the years, too, there have been modifications; for instance it is increasingly usual to speak of 'traditions' rather than of 'documents' when referring to an author's sources, in acknowledgement of the possibility that not only written records, but also material passed on by word of mouth and not previously written down, may have gone to make up the finished work. Yet the contribution of early literary and historical analysis to biblical insights was invaluable, and its techniques have become indispensable to any serious student.

Form criticism

This approach goes by a variety of names, among them 'form analysis', 'type criticism', and 'the form historical method'. It belongs mainly to the twentieth century, and it arose to some extent out of a recognition of the limitations of literary and historical analysis. When literary criticism has found out what it can about the authorship, date and sources of a book, a great many questions still remain unanswered about what is actually *in* the book, and it is at this point that form criticism takes a fresh look at the contents.

As we have seen, different types of literature exist side by side in the Old Testament; most books include prose and poetry, and the prose may range from law to apocalyptic whilst the poetry may be anything from a harvest song to a prophetic oracle. Similarly, the traditions or sources which make up a book or books may also be composite. For example, the oldest of the 'documentary' sources of the Pentateuch, known as J, or the

Yahwistic tradition (in it 'Yahweh' is the name used for God; J and Y represent the same letter in Hebrew), probably reached its recognizably final form as late as the tenth century B.C., centuries before it was incorporated into the Pentateuch as we have it, but also centuries after the events which it describes. Why were these particular traditions preserved when so much else was presumably lost? And what, in their far-off original setting, were they all about?

The form critic begins this journey into the past by selecting a number of examples of the same type of literature, say a particular kind of narrative, and looking at them side by side. He may see that these units are all constructed to a similar pattern – rather as if someone noticed for the first time that English fairy tales mostly begin 'Once upon a time' and end 'So they all lived happily ever after'. He will then consult the literature of neighbouring cultures, and may find there that similar stories are shaped in the same way. From this he might conclude that there was in the ancient Near East a special form for use when telling this kind of story, and that it would be employed on a certain kind of occasion. His further, and probably most difficult, task is then to try and discover what this occasion could have been; the technical term for it is *Sitz-im-Leben*, sometimes translated 'place-in-life', or perhaps more meaningfully 'life-situation'.

To see this method in operation we will look at the Psalter, upon which a great deal of form-critical work has been done. The Psalms are classified as hymns of praise to Yahweh, or thanksgivings, or laments (the last two sometimes communal, sometimes private), and as well as these main divisions there are smaller classifications and sub-divisions. Each type, or form, of poem has its own literary characteristics; for instance, a lament usually begins with an *invocation* to Yahweh, sometimes simply addressing him as 'Lord' or 'God', sometimes adding a further ascription:

> To thee, O LORD, I call;
> O my Rock, be not deaf to my cry (Ps. 28: 1).

Then comes the actual *complaint*; perhaps *illness*:

> Thy indignation has left no part of my body unscarred;
> there is no health in my whole frame because of my sin
> (Ps. 38: 3),

or *distress*:

> I am wearied with crying out, my throat is sore,
> my eyes grow dim as I wait for God to help me (Ps. 69: 3),

or *persecution by enemies*:

> Insolent men rise to attack me,
> ruthless men seek my life (Ps. 54: 3).

A *prayer* for relief may follow:

> Hear my prayer, O LORD;
> listen to my cry,
> hold not thy peace at my tears (Ps. 39: 12),

and often the psalmist makes a *vow*, to be kept if the prayer is heard and answered:

> So will I acclaim him with sacrifice before his tent
> and sing a psalm of praise to the LORD (Ps. 27: 6).

Although the lament reflects troubled circumstances, there is sometimes an *expression of confidence* that Yahweh will help:

> Well I know that I shall see the goodness of the LORD
> in the land of the living (Ps. 27: 13),

or even an anticipatory *hymn of thanksgiving*:

> For thou hast rescued me from death
> to walk in thy presence, in the light of life (Ps. 56: 13).

Of course, not all these elements are present in every lament, nor are they always in the same order, but enough of them recur for us to reconstruct the pattern. Similarly in a Babylonian prayer to the goddess Ishtar, dated about the seventh century B.C., we find the *invocation*:

> I pray to thee, O Lady of Ladies, goddess of goddesses,

and the *complaint*:

> I have cried to thee, suffering, wearied, and distressed, as thy servant,

and the *prayer*:

> See me, O my Lady; accept my prayers,
> Faithfully look upon me and hear my supplication.

What was the life-situation of the lament? When and where would complaint to Yahweh, whether personal or corporate, be presented in such a formal way? A comparison with parallels from other ancient cultures, and perhaps a look at set forms of prayer in later religious traditions, suggest that the likeliest occasion for use would be public worship. And since sacrifice is often mentioned, this worship must have taken place at any rate in the first instance in a shrine or sanctuary – indeed, the same kind of analysis applied to hymns and thanksgivings confirms the conclusion that most of the Psalter as we now have it originated in the liturgy of ancient Israel.

One might easily assume that the lament was used only during a time of trouble; in fact it could be in a sense retrospective, offered in a context of praise when the former sufferer looked back on the afflictions from which he had been delivered. Isa. 38: 10–20, beginning

I thought: In the prime of life I must pass away;
for the rest of my years I am consigned to the gates of Sheol,

is in the form of a lament, but verse 9 explains that it is attributed to king Hezekiah of Judah 'after his recovery from his illness'.

So there are three main elements in form criticism: the examination of material and recognition of the forms or literary types, the comparison with other literature, and the attempt to find the original life-situation of the various units. Like all methods, it has its limitations and drawbacks; for one thing, our view of the life-situation of any story or poem or law can only be a deduction from the available evidence, rather than a result of demonstrable proof. There are, too, dangers in taking the form-critical approach to excess. If, for instance, in the study of the Psalms we were to insist on fitting every psalm into one of a strictly limited number of categories and providing it willy-nilly with a life-situation connected with worship we would turn a flexible method into a rigid system and end by imposing a literary straitjacket on what was originally a living and vital growth. It stands to reason that some psalms will not conform to pattern, perhaps because they were not meant to be used in worship, or because they were individual compositions of a much later date.

Nor does form criticism supersede literary criticism, for when we have investigated the forms we are still concerned with the literary products of which they are a part. The Old Testament books are not a miscellaneous collection of remnants surviving from earlier ages; they are works in their own right, the outcome of political, social, religious and personal factors. The setting in which some of their contents originated is only one of these factors, and so we still need to concern ourselves with questions of date, authorship and composition.

But within its limits the form-critical approach has made a great contribution to our understanding of the Old Testament. It has helped to extend the bounds of our thought by taking into account the possibility that certain literary patterns were not peculiar to Israel but were held in common with her neighbours. In its concern with the spoken traditions which preceded the written word it has taken us back into the life of the people of the Old Testament and the customs and worship which lay at the heart of that life, and has enriched our appreciation of the beauty as well as of the background of some of the literature. It has been likened to the cleaning of a valuable picture, which reveals the splendour of the colours and brings to light details which for centuries have been unnoticed.

The traditio-historical approach
(redaction history)

Between the original life-situation of a story or poem or other literary unit and its incorporation into the Old Testament as we know it, there must often have been a gap of years or even centuries. The concern of the 'tradition historian' is with that period.

For example, it seems hardly likely that the stories in Genesis and Exodus were all written down whilst they were still in everyday use and then kept in sealed boxes until the final editor needed them; far more credible is the idea of them being handed down by word of mouth. Nor is it easy to think of this oral transmission, as it is called, as being purely mechanical, for this would conflict with what we understand of Israel's attitude to her own traditions. For instance, those great turning-points in Israelite history, the exodus and the wanderings in the wilderness, were events which when they happened radically affected the lives and destinies of the Israelites who were living at that time. But there is no evidence that they later became 'fossilized' stories which everyone knew by heart but regarded as having no immediate relevance. Instead, it seems as if each generation encountered these events, wrestled with their meaning, felt their influence, but above all was challenged by them in the contemporary situation. When the prophets invoked Yahweh as saying

> When Israel was a boy, I loved him;
> I called my son out of Egypt (Hos. 11: 1),

or

> I remember the unfailing devotion of your youth,
> the love of your bridal days,
> when you followed me in the wilderness,
> through a land unsown (Jer. 2: 2),

they expected an active response in terms of repentance and reformation, to the events which they recalled.

So Israelite history could never be relegated to the past; these and other living traditions, so well known that they could be cited without any explanation, must constantly have been *redacted* – that is, told and re-told, interpreted and reinterpreted, even expanded and contracted, to meet the needs of succeeding generations. And just as form criticism frequently concludes that many of its units originated in formal worship, so tradition, or *redaction*, history sees this worship down the centuries, with its continuing yet changing pattern of challenge and response, as the most likely setting for the repetition and adaptation of tradition.

How does this approach fit in with the sources, written or oral, suggested by literary analysis? In general terms, the answer is that whereas form criticism can co-exist with the possibility of such sources or even documents, tradition history may or may not be interested in them. Certainly they are regarded no longer as clearly definable, to be assigned to individual authors and editors, but rather as blocks of oral tradition which over a long period of time evolved and finally crystallized into literary form. Sometimes indeed the tradition historian goes further. For instance, one view of the Pentateuch is that it is the product of two distinct circles which used and transmitted the material. Genesis, Exodus, Leviticus and Numbers are known as the 'P-work', and originated in a 'priestly' circle which combined its own traditions with those of intersecting circles until the Tetrateuch (these first four Old Testament books) emerged. On the other hand the 'Deuteronomist history-work' (Deuteronomy and the following books, excluding Ruth, as far as the end of 2 Kings) was the offspring of quite different circles of traditionists, or 'tradents', who developed the view of events often called Deuteronomic, to be found in much of Deuteronomy and in parts of 1 and 2 Kings (for an example, see the comments on the fall of the Northern Kingdom in 2 Kings 17: 7–23, beginning 'All this happened to the Israelites because they had sinned against the LORD their God who brought them up from Egypt').

This particular theory cuts across the traditional sources of the Pentateuch, and even across the Pentateuch itself; it does not accept a number of parallel narratives existing side by side and finally combined by an editor, but instead proposes these two circles, each preserving and enlarging its own heritage until the Tetrateuch and the Deuteronomic history were completed. Even then the process was not finished, for after the Babylonian exile there was conflation; the story of the death of Moses ('P-work') was inserted into the Deuteronomic history and became Deut. 34. Such features as different names for God, of different ideas as to how he communicated with men, are no longer seen as indications of separate narrative strands, but may be thought to have been used by the same circle, according to what circumstances required.

On the other hand the traditio-historical approach may not be so entirely different from other methods of criticism as is sometimes suggested, for it seems in the end to get rid of one set of sources and editors and leave us with another. Even if no documents existed, the various traditions did, and were from time to time combined, and eventually the whole was edited into the literature as we know it. Someone, or some body of people, must have been responsible for this work. As with other approaches, we can see that this method has its own contribution to make to our understanding of the Old Testament, but equally that to some extent it is dependent on the others.

The determination of the text, of the literary composition of a passage and its historical background, of its component parts and their original life-situation, of the processes by which it was handed down and reached its final form, and of the meaning it had for those who handled it at all its stages; all this goes to make up the art or science of the interpretation of scripture, known as *hermeneutics*. And all has its part to play if we are to consider what relevance the Bible has for us today.

3

OTHER WRITINGS OF THE
JEWISH COMMUNITY

Background

The Old Testament canon, the name usually given to the collection of books in the Old Testament, is but a fraction of the Jewish literature surviving from biblical times. As many 'non-canonical' books are still intact; many more are known from fragments. Rabbi Akiba, the Jewish teacher who lived half a century after Jesus, called them the 'outside books', and defined them as 'Ben Sirach' (the Ecclesiasticus of the Apocrypha) 'and all written from then onwards'; he condemned those who read them. Ben Sirach was written in the first decade of the second century B.C., and the Jewish community in Palestine was finally destroyed some three centuries later. The writings of these momentous years are known as the Apocrypha and Pseudepigrapha, and they were all, with the exception of the book of Daniel, excluded from the Hebrew Old Testament.

These books have been divided into two groups as a result of differences in the manner of their preservation. Some of the books were highly esteemed by Greek-speaking Jews, and had been included in their collection known as the Septuagint. This was a translation, originally of the first five books of the Old Testament only, but subsequently of the entire Hebrew canon and more besides. Its limits were not defined during the period under consideration, and it remained amorphous even after the Church adopted it as the basis of the Greek

75

Bible (see chapter 4). Thus the early Church preserved some of the books which the Rabbis (the Jewish teachers and scholars) had excluded. These are known today as the *apocryphal* books, a name probably first used by Jerome in the fourth century when he distinguished these 'books of the Church' from the 'books of the (Hebrew) canon'.

The other group of books has had a more precarious history. Some were translated into Greek and appear in Septuagint manuscripts; some were taken over by Oriental churches speaking Coptic, Ethiopic and Syriac, who translated these texts into their own languages, so that, long after the Hebrew or Aramaic originals had been lost, the books could still be read. Some remain only as fragments; many, doubtless, have been lost in the course of two thousand years. Those which remain are known as the *Pseudepigrapha*, which means 'writings under a pseudonym' – scarcely an apt title, since of their number 1 Enoch is the only book thus written. The strange style and content of these books have led to their frequent neglect. Discoveries near the Dead Sea at Qumran, however, testify to their importance amongst some sections of the Jewish community during these turbulent years, which were crucial for Judaism and formative for Christianity.

The times in which they were written, and their exclusion from the Hebrew Old Testament, are all that these works have in common. Represented in the Apocrypha are the two types of wisdom literature (namely collections of proverbs, and moral tales), prose history, literature more akin to apocalyptic than to any other known form, and a pious pseudepigraph. The Pseudepigrapha are even more varied: psalms, a diatribe on the

Law, legends from the third century B.C. (when Palestine was ruled by Egypt), apocalyptic, and a revised version of Genesis. The official reason for the exclusion of so diverse a body of literature was its too recent origin, but there were almost certainly other reasons. Many of the books indicate that the Judaism of their authors was very different from that of the Rabbis. Little is known of this non-Pharisaic Judaism; even the first-century Jewish historian Josephus, whose works are often the only source of information for the period, was a Pharisee, and therefore not unbiased. Much of the thought of the Jewish community of these years has been irretrievably lost. Only a tentative reconstruction is possible, and even then it must be remembered that the non-canonical Jewish books were preserved, and altered, by Christian hands.

The earlier apocalyptic writings

Of the literature represented in the Apocrypha and Pseudepigrapha, most is of types well known from either the Old Testament or contemporary Greek writers: wisdom, proverbs and psalms being examples of the former; diatribes of the latter. Apocalyptic, on the other hand, has survived almost exclusively in non-canonical books, and the few instances in the canon are not entirely representative of the scope or style of the mass of apocalyptic literature, for it was only the milder works which the Rabbis saw fit to include. Daniel is one such canonical work, but apocalyptic traits are discernible in much older books, for instance parts of Ezekiel, Isaiah and Zechariah (see p. 53). The oldest of the extant Apocalypses is *1 Enoch*, whose earliest parts were probably compiled at the beginning of the second century B.C.

The writers of this Apocalypse drew widely upon older material, the *Book of Noah,* and many other non-biblical legends, some of which are similar to the myths of Greece and Mesopotamia. Scholars have argued that apocalyptic was written by Jews excessively influenced by these foreign ideas. The outlook and content of these books showed only the most extreme examples of this assimilation, and were therefore unsuitable for general reading. Were this the whole truth, there would be no difficulty in harmonizing such thought with that of orthodox Judaism. Problems arise when one considers the historical and social setting of these writings. It becomes very clear that they were not the expression of a compromising minority. Apocalyptic flourished in the troubled years of the Maccabees, and in the time of the last struggles against Rome by the Zealots, the Jews who actively resisted outside political control.

1 Enoch, the earliest, is also the longest of these works. It is a typical Apocalypse, written under a pseudonym (the Enoch of Gen. 5: 21-4), and is usually considered in five sections (chapters 6-35, 36-71, 72-82, 83-90, 91-105). The second of these is thought to be a Christian work, or at least much altered by Christian hands. It is the only section not yet found at Qumran, where parts of ten Aramaic manuscripts of Enoch have been identified. The rest of the book deals with the problem of evil. The revolt of the angels (Gen. 6) was the beginning of evil. 'The whole earth has been corrupted by the works taught by Azazel...who revealed the eternal secrets of heaven, which men were striving to learn' (En. 9: 10). 'As men perished they cried to heaven' (En. 8). At the End the fallen angels would go to the 'abyss of fire' and the righteous escape to the Golden Age, when creation would

be released from daemonic corruption. Words reminiscent of Amos describe the sinners, 'rulers' who collaborated with 'oppressors' to 'rob and devour' (En. 103). They were assured of punishment. 'I know a mystery...ye shall have no peace.' The righteous were promised 'goodness and joy and glory', 'in recompense for their labours'. All present turmoils were the foreordained preliminaries of the End. 'Read in the heavenly tablets' – it was just a matter of time.

Parts of the book were written at very different times, some as much as a century after the Maccabees (that is, fifty years before Christ). But the work must be considered as a whole, for the author did not merely collect an anthology of unrelated ideas.

Nor were these the problems of a Jew steeped in foreign thought. It was the very fundamentals of Judaism which were incompatible with the contemporary situation. The refusal to compromise made new explanations necessary, and in these, the ideas were inextricably bound to the bizarre imagery of apocalyptic. One cause of controversy was the alteration of the calendar. 1 Enoch has ten chapters on this theme. 'The Luminaries of the heaven, the relations of each...Uriel the holy angel, who is their guide, showed me...all their laws, exactly as they are, all the years of the world, unto eternity' (En. 72: 1 ff.). The control of the calendar was very important (see also p. 84). Jeroboam (1 Kings 12: 32) had assumed this right, and Rabbi Johannan ben Zakkai made regulation of the calendar a priority in A.D. 70, after the collapse of the old regime, when Rome put down the Jewish revolt. Samaritans, and many Jewish sects, were united upon, or divided by, this very issue. To tamper with the plan for the year was to upset the natural order. 'In the days of the sinners, the years shall be shortened...and all things on the earth shall alter, and the rain be kept back' (En. 80: 2 ff.). Since the agricultural cycle was as dependent upon ritual as upon rainfall, any corruption or disruption was seen, especially in rural areas, as the intrusion of evil. They saw that the stars which determined the months were out of phase; the heavens, as in the time of Azazel, were in revolt. Thus, too, the apocalyptist linked astrology with social evils. 'Owing to them men shall be at fault' (En. 82: 5). Since a tradition as old as the prophets also links political powers with the stars (Isa. 14: 12), a picture emerges of attempts to relate astrology to climate and crops, political upheaval, and social unrest, all illustrated by, or perhaps dependent upon, the oldest strata of folk lore.

The events of the three centuries before the fall of Jerusalem had destroyed any optimistic theology of history. God could only be working despite world events, no longer through them. The apocalyptists attempted to see through to the real meaning of life, by resorting to a type of mystical experience which fortified them against life's inconsistencies, and entrusted to them a panoramic vision of history stretching beyond the present crises into the Messianic age. All was foreseen; all could be known.

The later apocalyptic writings

The last two centuries B.C. produced many other works like the Apocalypses, for instance the Sibylline oracles, the Testaments of the Twelve Patriarchs, Jubilees, or the Psalms of Solomon, but each was tangential to apocalyptic proper. The majority of extant Apocalypses were written in the first century A.D. All have been edited by Christians. Their original themes are still clear, even if their original setting is not. They are concerned with the problem of evil, and the outcome of history.

The Assumption of Moses, only partially extant, extols righteous martyrs, and thus gives a clue to its origins. 'For if we do this and die, our blood shall be avenged before the Lord. Then his Kingdom shall appear, throughout all his creation' (Assumption of Moses 9: 7 ff.). Moses reveals the history of Israel, culminating in the woes which precede the Judgement. The End would be heralded by the disruption of all creation. Chapter 10 is very like parts of Revelation. 'Then thou, O Israel, shalt be happy' (Assumption of Moses 10: 8), 'For God will go forth, who hath foreseen all things' (Assumption of Moses 12: 13).

The Apocalypse of Moses (there are many versions of this, under more appropriate names, for instance *Life of Adam and Eve*) shows how serious speculation about man and his lot was frequently cast in the form of a pious legend about biblical figures (called Haggadah, from the Hebrew *haggid*, to report, or explain; see also p. 169). The story of Eden, heavily embellished, asks what 'Man in the image of God' really implies. Satan's jealousy causes the rift between man and God; man's status in creation is his salvation. 'Pardon him, Father of all, for he is in thine image' (Apocalypse of Moses 35: 2).

The Secrets of Enoch (Slavonic Enoch, so called because it survives in two versions in Slavonic, an ancient form of Slavic speech) is of disputed date. It deals with the problem of the calendar, and, like 1 Enoch, gives a revelation of history as the result of a mystical ascent. Exhortation to lead a good life is the main theme; God's people would have their own reward.

The Apocalypse of Ezra (2 Esdras), of which only

chapters 3–14 are thought to be Jewish, is very similar to 2 Baruch. (The latter probably drew upon the former rather than vice versa.) Chapter 14 is the well-known legend of Ezra's dictating the scriptures after the fall of Jerusalem. Twenty-four books were for general reading, seventy secret books were only for the wise – the apocalyptists' charter! In the form of Ezra's seven visions in Babylon, the writer questions the relationship between the Law and man's impieties. 'They received the commandments but did not keep them, they accepted the law but violated it' (2 Esdras 7: 72). 'A grain of the evil seed was sown in the heart of Adam' (2 Esdras 4: 30).

All these first-century writers asked, 'Why has Israel been made a byword among the Gentiles?' (2 Esdras 4: 23) – the old problem of the exilic writers. Both ages denied that punishment was inherited. 'Each of us has been the Adam of his own soul', that is, each has himself disobeyed God of his own free will (2 Baruch 54: 19, cp. Ezek. 33: 10 ff., Jer. 31: 29 ff.), but the later writers hoped for an after-life to redress the balance.

The Testament of Abraham, although apocalyptic in outlook, is not addressing a crisis in history. Abraham sees the seven millennia and the three judgements, but the writer is interested more in the fate of individual souls than in the future of the nation.

The Martyrdom of Isaiah was probably not a Jewish work, although based on Jewish legends.

It is not easy to decide which section of the Jewish community wrote such literature. The centuries of stress produced a very kaleidoscope of feuds and alliances, both theological and political. At one time it was attributed to the early Pharisees, but the Zadokite Fragment (see below) could well cast doubt upon this.

Other views of the Law

The Zadokite Fragment, also known as the Damascus Document, usually designated C.D. (Cairo Damascus Document), is extant in some mediaeval manuscripts found in Cairo and in fragments from Qumran. It tells of a strange persecuted community dedicated to the Law, who had 'like the blind, been groping after the way for many years' (C.D. 1: 6), and had been led by a 'Teacher of Righteousness' to 'Damascus', where they awaited the final destruction of evil men, and the appearance of the 'Messiah of Aaron and Israel'. It is generally thought to be anti-Pharisaic. The causes of friction were differing views on the permanence and status of the Law. The Pharisees spoke 'against the statutes of the covenant of God, saying, "they are not established"' (C.D. 7: 13). The persecuted community disagreed on the role of the oral Law, certain liberal marriage laws, and on Sabbath and calendar calculations. All Israel except these 'Zadokites' had erred in 'his holy Sabbath and glorious festivals' (C.D. 5: 2), and furthermore the Zadokites disliked the Pharisees' support of the Davidic house. Opposition to these Pharisaic traits is common in the apocalyptic books of the first and second centuries B.C., but the acceptance of 'angels', and the idea of an after-life (the usual grounds for attributing apocalyptic to the Pharisees), is nowhere mentioned in the Zadokite document as a distinctive or unpopular trait.

Closely linked with the Zadokite Fragment is the Book of Jubilees, the source of some of the Damascus community's laws, and usually dated during, or slightly before, the Maccabaean revolt. This work reveals more of the religious thought of the 'rest' of the Jewish community than any other book. The author is unknown; scholars used to think that he was a Pharisee of the reign of John Hyrcanus. Recently this has been modified. Jubilees is a revision of Genesis, adapted so as to emphasize the status and everlasting validity of the Law. Traditional lore is used to illustrate biblical material, and the result is known as a *Midrash*. (See p. 169. Chronicles is a Midrash of Samuel–Kings.) The book is the work of one author, stating one consistent point of view. The Kingdom of God would be inaugurated only when 'the children shall begin to study the laws...and return to the paths of righteousness...and there shall be no Satan, or evil destroyer, and all their days shall be days of blessing and healing' (Jub. 23: 26 ff.).

Moses was given not only the Law, but also a panoramic view of God's purpose, inscribed on heavenly tablets, 'from the beginning of creation, until my sanctuary has been built for all eternity' (Jub. 1: 28). The Law was instituted long before it was revealed to Moses: 'the festival was celebrated in heaven from the day of creation until the day of (its revelation to) Noah' (Jub. 6: 18), and thus was an integral and immutable part of creation. The whole Patriarchal saga was revised to show this progressive revelation.

The other main theme is the calendar: 'On the heavenly tablets the division of days is ordained' (Jub. 6: 35). The author insists on the use of the old priestly calendar as used by the Enoch literature (p. 79), and adapts his histories to fit. Scholars have argued that this calendar was only speculative, and was never actually used. The 'priestly' part of the Old Testament also formalized sagas to fit this same solar calendar. The main events in the account of Noah's flood, for example, are all on a

Wednesday according to the old calendar (Gen. 8: 5, 13, 14), as are most of the events in Jubilees' account of the Patriarchs. It is unlikely that this was mere astrological speculation, for it led to bitter conflict, and even to bloodshed. The Jubilees calendar was used at Qumran, but not, apparently, by the Pharisees or in Jerusalem. (For example, Qumran, Jubilees and the Sadducees said that no festival could fall on the Sabbath; the Pharisees disagreed.) The actual name 'Jubilees' comes from the author's schematizing of history into periods of forty-nine years, known as jubilees, a method also used by Samaritans in their Tolidah (a work of disputed date, which has many other points of contact with Jubilees – for example, the ages of the Patriarchs).

Jubilees also provides a wealth of material from non-canonical sources, showing the affinities of this, and similar, books. The accounts of the origins of some festivals are not the well-known stories of the Old Testament. The Day of Atonement, for example (Jub. 38: 18 ff.), is penitence for the betrayal of Joseph. Since much of another work, the Testaments of the Twelve Patriarchs, is also on this theme, the author's sympathies are revealed. Jubilees' picture of Moses is like the Samaritan tradition, and much of the illustrative material comes from the stock of peripheral legend common to the Septuagint, Philo the first-century Egyptian Jew, and the Palestinian Targum (one of the Aramaic paraphrases of the Old Testament; see pp. 154–6). Even the text on which it is based is nearer to the Genesis of the Septuagint or the Samaritan version than to the Massoretic. The *Halakah* of Jubilees (details of the application of the Law; from the Hebrew *halak*, to go – used in the sense of way; then of 'guidance'; see p. 169) has more in common with that of the Sadducees and of the Samaritans than that of the Pharisees. Such a kaleidoscope was the political and theological scene in Palestine that this can indicate no more than a non-Pharisaic author. The Messianic hope, usually an indication of a non-canonical author's sympathies, is not clearly defined in Jubilees. Most scholars detect a priestly Messiah, another non-Pharisaic trait.

The translation of the Law

There is another book on the status of the Law; a strange legend set in the reign of Ptolemy II (285–247 B.C.) in Alexandria. The *Letter of Aristeas* (more correctly a narrative) tells how the Hebrew scriptures were translated into Greek for the great library at Alexandria. The work was done by seventy-two elders (hence Septuagint, from the Latin for seventy), who, working separately, produced identical translations. The miraculous version was accepted as authoritative. Josephus records what is probably the truth underlying this legend (*Antiquities* 13, 4, 4). The Jews and Samaritans had both settled in Alexandria in large numbers; disputes arose as to which was the rightful recipient of the royal bounties, and this involved establishing whose version of the scriptures was correct. The official recognition granted to one particular version as a result of this gave rise to the 'Aristeas' legend. It must not be thought that the translation of the scriptures into Greek was a single operation. Aristobulus, a contemporary of the Maccabees, said that some of the Law was in Greek by Plato's time, although this is probably just propaganda, since the Jews of this time were very keen to show from the superior age of the Torah (the Law) that Greek philosophers had merely copied, and copied badly.

The Septuagint as we know it today has obviously come from many translations, and the Hebrew text on which it was based was not that of the later Massoretes. An older Hebrew text, such as underlies Jubilees and other non-canonical works, was used. Josephus used it; it was widely known. Although, in the words of Ecclesiasticus, 'it is impossible for a translator to find precise equivalents for the original Hebrew' (Ecclus., preface), some of the differences between the Septuagint and the Hebrew text come from implied references to the lore and legend which are the stuff of so much non-canonical literature, especially apocalyptic. The generation of scholars which excluded these writings also made another Greek translation of the Old Testament, Aquila's (see pp. 148–9).

The Jewish reaction to Greek ideas

The Letter of Aristeas, besides describing the feat of translation, gives a valuable account of the land of Palestine, the city of Jerusalem and the temple, and follows this with a discussion between Jews and Greeks on the merits of Law and philosophy. The former (ch. 31) is of 'divine origin, full of wisdom and free from blemish', and (ch. 127) 'the good life consists in the keeping of the enactments of the Law'. 'The whole system aims at righteous relationships between man and man' (ch. 169). The Law is vastly superior to the wisdom of other cultures (ch. 140), 'leading Egyptian priests to call us men of God'. The more obscure parts of it are allegorized, lest rational Greeks be offended. Yahweh, 'the Lord and master of the universe', is none other than 'Zeus, though we call him by a different name' (ch. 15). In view of the bitter conflicts between Maccabees and Seleucids, Jews and Romans, over the spread of Greek ideas and the Roman deities, such a statement is indeed remarkable, since it shows how some Jews reacted to this Hellenism. The Letter of Aristeas, with its sophisticated 'after dinner' discussion on ethics, is one of the many pieces of Jewish propaganda. Only the material is Jewish. All else is Greek. Other extant literature shows that such assimilation was common only among the educated. Ironically, their reaction was to assert the superiority of Jewish culture, by re-expressing it in Greek forms!

There is a great dispute as to the date of the Letter. The latter part of the second century is suggested by a number of scholars, and this was certainly a time when such propaganda flourished. Artapanus was another writer of the second century who exalted Israel at the expense of Egypt. An Ezekiel wrote Greek tragedy on Jewish themes; a Philo (not the philosopher) wrote epic poetry, and the wisdom writers of Judaism borrowed ideas from Greece, which had a profound effect on this ancient Hebrew tradition, as can be seen in the Wisdom of Solomon.

There was, however, another reaction to Hellenism. In such a cosmopolitan society, there were the less educated folk who could not make a sophisticated assessment of each other's ideas. Each adopted the folklore of the other into his own core of unwritten tradition, without losing those features of thought which were characteristic of his own culture. The most outstanding example of this, the Testament of Joseph, is part of the *Testaments of the Twelve Patriarchs*.

The Testaments are linked both in form and date to Jubilees – traditionally they purport to be the last words of the sons of Jacob, just as Jubilees reports the dying exhortations of Abraham and Isaac. The work is pre-occupied with morality, a comprehensive self-condemnation. Society was saturated with undesirable Greek ways. The writer's spirit is thoroughly Jewish, and so high was the tone of his teaching, that the book was long thought to be a Christian composition, or to have been edited by Christians beyond recognition. Since fragments of two closely related works have been found at Qumran (a Hebrew Testament of Naphtali and an Aramaic Testament of Levi), there is now little reason to doubt the Jewish origin of the bulk of the Testaments.

Four are especially interesting. The Testament of Levi tells of Levi's transportation in the Enoch manner to visions of the upper world and the heavenly temple. He is told the significance of each of the priestly vestments. The Testament of Judah has many of the non-biblical tales which are told in Jubilees. It also recounts the incident of Judah and Tamar (Gen. 38: 12 ff.) and says, significantly, of Judah's claim to the monarchy as a result, 'I gave away my staff, the stay of my tribe; and my girdle, my power; and my diadem, the glory of my kingdom' (Test. Judah 15: 3). There are two versions of the Testament of Naphtali: the Greek, part of the Testaments proper, which has also been partially re-covered in Hebrew from Qumran, and a completely independent Hebrew version of much later date. The greatest difference between them is their attitude to Joseph. The later work hates him, the earlier does not. As in 1 Enoch and Jubilees, the origin of evil is linked with the fallen angels, and contemporary disorders are the result of disrupting both the heavenly bodies and the cycle of nature. The Testament of Joseph, perhaps the most important of the four, is a moral tale in truly Semitic style. Although many motifs are Greek, the outlook is that of the less cultured Jew who absorbed foreign tales in his cosmopolitan society, but none of its values or style. A comparison with Josephus's version of the Joseph story shows this best (*Antiquities* 5, 2, 77). Whereas the Testament portrays the Divine as grotesque and fearful, Josephus talks in terms of the beauty of the Greek deities. The theme of the Testament is unique. The other brothers are penitent for their attitude towards Joseph; he illustrates the triumph of virtue. The work in its Greek form is propaganda on behalf of Joseph, as well as a condemnation of contemporary society.

Popular tales

The literature of these centuries affords other examples of such moral tales. They are frequently referred to as a development of the old 'wisdom' literature, and are often foreign tales recast in the mould of Jewish piety.

Tobit is one such book; set in the eastern Diaspora (the non-Palestinian communities of Jews) after the fall of Samaria, it tells of the good works of a pious Jew and his eventual reward. An angel defeats a wicked demon, enabling his son to marry the girl of his choice. The story reflects the conditions of eastern Jewry at the beginning of the second century, and shows the great importance of the Law in everyday life. 'I, Tobit, made truth and righteousness my lifelong guide; I did many acts of charity for my kinsmen...at the festivals I was the only one to make the frequent journey to Jerusalem... with the firstfruits of crops and herds...and I gave them to the priests of Aaron's line' (Tobit 1: 3, 6).

Judith is another; set in Jerusalem in the time of Nebuchadnezzar, it tells of a Jewess who makes advances to an enemy general in order to assassinate him. The tale, with its scrupulous regard for the Law (Judith, whilst preparing to entice the foreigner, will eat only her own ritually pure, or kosher, food), and great national loyalty, reveals the spirit of second-century Judaism, conscious of its superiority and confident that good must eventually defeat evil Gentiles.

Attached to the book of Daniel in the Septuagint are two more moral tales, *Daniel and Susanna*, and *Daniel, Bel and the Snake*. Each tells of the wisdom of Daniel, and of his triumph over the credulity of the Babylonians. One tale tells of a girl wrongly accused of adultery, who is proved innocent by Daniel's clever cross-examination. The other tells how he unmasked the priests of Bel, proving that their cult was mere deceit.

The national pride and confidence which such tales depict was not the whole picture; anti-Semitic feelings, especially in centres with a large Jewish quarter, were not unknown. *3 Maccabees* (an ill-named book, since it has nothing to do with the Maccabees) tells of such troubles in Alexandria. The book purports to be a history of the last decades of the third century B.C., and describes God's miraculous intervention to save his people, and prevent the violation of his temple. Ptolemy IV (221–204 B.C.) had tried to force idolatry upon Egyptian Jewry; resisting the king's threats, they were three times saved from trampling by the king's elephants. The king relented, and a festival of thanksgiving was instituted, probably equivalent to Purim, the festival of eastern Jewry to celebrate their deliverance by the action of Esther.

Judaism for the Greek world

The Jewish community made many attempts in these years to commend itself to the Gentile world. Besides trying to prove the greater age, and therefore superiority, of Jewish culture, its writers also adopted the styles of popular Hellenistic writing in order to attract a wider circle of readers. A large body of literature known as the *Sibylline Oracles* is the strangest example of this. Some four thousand lines are extant, of which three 'books' (3, 4, 5) are certainly of Jewish origin. The Sibyl was originally a prophetess of the Greeks and Romans, mentioned as early as the sixth century B.C. by the philosopher Heracleitus. Her cryptic utterances, often foreboding doom and destruction, were revered by the ancient pagan world. Later writers had formalized and extended this style, so as to include pseudonymous surveys of world history with predictions of its outcome, similar to the histories of Daniel and 1 Enoch. The Jewish writers saw in these writings a powerful medium of communication. The Sibyl became Noah's daughter-in-law, and her oracles retold the history of the world. Book 3, written by an Egyptian Jew in the third century, incorporates the new with the old. The giants, the off-spring of the fallen angels in the apocalyptic tradition, become the Titans. Zeus plays a prominent part. Despite this, the oracle's main purpose is to condemn idolatry! 'Ye men that bear the form that God did mould in his own image...why do ye not walk in the straight path...mindful of eternal creation?' (3: 8). Contemporary evil springs from this idolatry; the writer's analysis cannot fail to remind one of Paul's similar discourse in Romans. The bulk of the book is the cryptic condemnation of foreign powers, and the prediction of the eventual triumph of right, namely Judaism.

A second work in Greek style is of much later date and very different content. *4 Maccabees*, written at about the turn of the era, is a discourse in the manner of the Stoic philosophers on 'inspired or godly reason'. The Jewish Law was the only certain way to achieve the Stoic virtues. Under its guidance, the passions, which Stoics regarded as the product of wrong thinking, and therefore degrading, could be accepted and re-directed. 'For in the day that God created man, he implanted in him his passions and inclinations and also the mind...to which he gave the Law; by which if a man order himself, he shall reign over a kingdom temperate, just, virtuous and brave' (2: 21). 'Reason, through the Law, is able to overcome even hatred' (2: 12). 'None can extirpate a malevolent disposition, but reason can be his powerful ally against being swayed by malevolence' (3: 4).

Such high ideals are illustrated by gruesome tales of the endurance of the Maccabaean martyrs, and the profound effect which their sufferings had on both contemporaries and subsequent generations.

The influence of 4 Maccabees extended far beyond Alexandria; the fourth-century Fathers Gregory Nazianzen and John Chrysostom had it in mind when they wrote on martyrdom. Though struggling 'before the days of grace', the Maccabees were an inspiration to Christians in their suffering.

Wise men in an age of change

Wisdom literature is represented in the Apocrypha by two books: *Ecclesiasticus* and the *Wisdom of Solomon*, although there are wisdom traits in other works, such as

1 Enoch's strange masquerade of history in animal fables, and the Testaments' picture of Joseph.

Ecclesiasticus (not to be confused with Ecclesiastes) is unique in that its preface tells how it was translated into Greek. It was written at the beginning of the second century B.C., and was translated from Hebrew by the author's grandson for the Jews of Alexandria. The preface says that it is a 'book ... on the themes of discipline and wisdom'. Like the book of Proverbs, it has its exhortations and pithy sayings, but it also has hymns about the glory of God in creation, and a review of the great figures of Israel's traditions.

The author reflects second-century life in a Jerusalem well acquainted with foreign ways. His was a refined gentility, courteous, non-committal, and acutely aware of his aristocratic station in life. 'A scholar's wisdom comes of ample leisure...how can a man become wise who guides the plough...and talks only about cattle?' (38: 24, 25). 'They cannot expound moral or legal principles and are not ready with maxims' (38: 33). How different from the later Rabbis' pride in their crafts!

The book is a collection of the exhortations traditional to 'wisdom', but is more distinctively Jewish than its canonical predecessors. The national heritage is a source of great pride and security in the cosmopolitan society of the time. Great men of Judaism are heroes in the Greek manner; the enquiring agnosticism of Ecclesiastes and Job are completely overlooked. With confidence it could be said 'was anyone who trusted the Lord ever disappointed?' (2: 10), and yet the interpretation of the Law was far from narrow. In anticipation of the later Rabbis, the writer could say that almsgiving and good deeds were the equivalent of temple sacrifice, for 'to

heed the commandments is to sacrifice a thank-offering'
(35: 1). In view of his admiration for the priesthood,
inseparable from his aristocratic birth, such liberality
speaks highly of some aspects of pre-Maccabaean Jerusalem. The Hebrew (but not the Greek) of chapter 51
extols the Zadokite priesthood (Zadok was appointed
priest by king David, and his descendants were generally
considered to be the only legitimate priests – cp. Ezek. 44:
15), and almost all chapter 50 is a paean to the last great
high priest, Simon, who held office, 219-199 B.C. 'How
glorious he was... like the sun shining on the temple of
the Most High' (50: 5 ff.).

The author of the *Wisdom of Solomon* lived in Egypt.
His thoughts were based on traditional wisdom, but so
embellished with the ideas and style of contemporary
Greek culture, that Jerome condemned the book as
'stinking of Greek eloquence'. Earlier wisdom writers, of
whom the author of Ecclesiastes was the most pessi-
mistic, had asked how man's miserable lot could be
compatible with a just God. The apocalyptists had had the
same problem when confronted with the problem of the
martyrs. A life beyond was the answer, either resurrection
or immortality. The writer of the Wisdom of Solomon
chose the latter, a Greek idea, and in his second chapter
dismissed Ecclesiastes' pessimism. Thus ended a long
tradition. The corruptible body, as the prison of the pre-
existent soul, replaced the old idea of prosperity and
fulfilment in this world as the sign of God's favour. The
problems of injustice disappeared.

Wisdom itself changed. Originally it had been those
insights into human life which were passed on to the
young. Later these were identified with the Law, Wisdom, 'the covenant-book of God Most High' (Ecclus.

24: 23). Now it had become the universal spirit, 'pure effluence from the glory of the Almighty' (Wisd. of Sol. 7: 25). All Israel's history was reviewed to show wisdom's special concern for God's people. 'She brought them over the Red Sea' (Wisd. of Sol. 10: 18), and drowned the Egyptians.

Philo's works show the final development of this idea. The Law took on some of these aspects of wisdom, and he demonstrated to his Greek readers that the Law was perfect because it was the perfect expression of the natural Law. The Wisdom of Solomon also foreshadows Romans 2 in seeing idolatry as the essential perversion of the God-given order. 'For the worship of idols... is the beginning, cause, and end of every evil' (Wisd. of Sol. 14: 27). Moral decay and the dislocating of creation are inseparable. The apocalyptists, far from the academic life of Alexandria, drew the same conclusion.

Jewish resistance to Greek ideas

Whilst the Jews of Alexandria were absorbing Greek ideas, and expounding Judaism in the language of Hellenism, the Jews of Palestine were developing that great body of learning which was eventually systematized as the *Mishnah*. Far from being re-expressed in contemporary ideas, the Law, which was much discussed in its application to all aspects of daily life, became protected by a 'fence' of learned interpretation. Eventually the Rabbis' rules and interpretation became binding, and were handed on as part of the tradition. Sixty-three books of this tradition, known as Halakah, were collected. *Pirke Aboth* ('the chapters of the Fathers') was included, but unlike the rest of the Mishnah, it is not Halakah. It is a list of the great men who developed that tradition, together with the more famous sayings of each scholar. Many resemble the proverbs of the old wisdom schools: 'keep far from an evil neighbour, and consort not with the wicked' (Pirke Aboth 1: 7). Others show the deep piety of Rabbinic Judaism: 'Beloved is man in that he was created in the image of God. Greater love was it that made known to him that he was made in the image' (3: 19).

The first chapter of the work is probably the most important. It traces the growth of the Law through Israel's history, and shows clearly the need of the Jewish community to root their present firmly in their past. The Law came through Moses, the prophets, and the Men of the Great Synagogue (the traditional name for Ezra and his associates). It was passed on through Simon the Just, who was both the last of these men and the first of the scholar saints of Judaism who were to build that 'fence for the Law' which enabled it to survive the catastrophes of the Roman era.

New poetry

Just as the Law was extended during these centuries, so too were some of the poetic forms familiar from the Davidic Psalter. A collection of eighteen poems has survived in Greek and Syriac, although scholars usually assume there was a Hebrew original. They are known as the *Psalms of Solomon*, because king Solomon was legendary as a writer of songs (1 Kings 4: 32). Unlike the Wisdom of Solomon, the poems are not a contrived pseudepigraph. Many psalm-styles from the Old Testament are easily recognized; there are the laments, hymns and thanksgivings, much intermingled to suit the developed style of the later psalmist. A mood of reflection and retrospection dominates the poems: 'He reflected not that he was a man, and recognized not that it is God who is great' (2: 32). Half of the psalms are the outpourings of a 'righteous' man against 'sinners': 'O Lord deliver my soul from the lawless and wicked man' (12: 1). These sinners are 'insolent in prosperity', 'polluters of holy things', 'deceitful in their speech', and adulterers in their private lives. They have abandoned the Davidic monarchy, and the psalmist, whilst rejoicing at the fall of the Hasmonaeans (the Jewish rulers who came to power after the Maccabaean revolt), sees in their successors, the Romans, a terrible, but justified, punishment upon Jerusalem. The whole work is steeped in the prophetic imagery of judgement, especially Isaiah's. Fallen Jerusalem echoes fallen Babylon of old, 'her beauty cast upon the ground'. The future Davidic king (17: 32 ff.) is the fulfilment of all the Isaianic hopes. Jeremiah's cup of destruction has been drained – 'a cup of undiluted wine that they might become drunken' (8: 15) – and the hated foreign ruler dies, in Ezekiel's manner, 'slain on the mountains of Egypt' (2: 30). It is not known who wrote these psalms. Assertions that Pharisees wrote them condemning Sadducees are less confident since the findings at Qumran. There are echoes of the language of the apocalyptists, and of part of the Zadokite Fragment. Historical allusions suggest that the poems were written in the middle of the first century B.C.

Tales of conflict

All these 'other writings' had one thing in common: the troubled times in which they were written. It has been suggested that during the periods of Persian and Egyptian rule there was no attempt to impose new religious or cultural ideas. Power and peace, trade and taxes were all that mattered. There was no challenge to Judaism, and so no literature of polemical or apologetic nature was produced. Very little is known of the centuries preceding the rise of the Seleucids, those Syrian rulers who were allotted part of the empire of Alexander the Great. They conquered Palestine in 198 B.C.; one generation of goodwill towards Judaism was followed by many years of bitter conflict. They attempted to eradicate Judaism – whether for cultural or political reasons is not clear.

Elsewhere Hellenism was little more than a cultural challenge to be met with words; in Palestine it became a threat to Judaism's very existence, and was met with violence. The years of resistance began with the Maccabees (166 B.C.) and ended with the final Roman conquest (A.D. 70). Originally the aim was religious freedom; it became clear that without political freedom this was impossible, and so the struggle was for independence. There are various accounts of these campaigns; Josephus made a chronicle of them in 'The Wars of the Jews'. He was a Pharisee, and these beliefs, together with his ambiguous attitude to the resistance movements, make it impossible for him to convey the spirit of the times, even though his is the greatest volume of facts available.

1 and 2 Maccabees tell of the early years of fighting. They are not consecutive volumes, but two overlapping accounts of the deeds of the Maccabees. Scholars have questioned the relationship between them, since they do not give events in the same order, and 2 Maccabees sets out to abridge the five volumes of one 'Jason of Cyrene', an author otherwise unknown (2: 19). The similarities probably arise from Jason and 1 Maccabees using the

same oral tradition, and the differences from the rough hands of the revisers.

1 Maccabees has an atmosphere like that of Judges or 1 and 2 Samuel. The Lord again leads the armies of Israel. The pioneers of the resistance are typically Hebrew, brave and skilful fighters, yet deeply pious and dedicated to the Law. 'We are fighting for our lives and our religion. Heaven will crush them before our eyes' (3:21). In their political acts they were both shrewd and practical. The author conveys the spirit of the times by the speeches which he attributes to the main characters. Yahweh's actions in the past are recalled, and his miraculous interventions to save his people. Jerusalem, desecrated by foreigners whose 'language was friendly, but full of guile' (1:30), is like the ruins of Jeremiah's time.

This book was written at least half a century after the events it describes. It closes with a reference to the Chronicles of Hyrcanus, which would have been completed towards the end of his period of office – 104 B.C. The original language was Hebrew. Origen, the third-century Christian writer from Egypt, says it was called 'The Book of the House of Sabaniel', an as yet inexplicable name.

2 Maccabees reminds one of the literature of the Diaspora, the folk tales of Babylonian and Egyptian Jewry, such as Tobit or 3 Maccabees. It is history embellished in the popular manner. The Seleucid official sent to remove the temple treasure is punished by a terrible apparition, which beats him senseless, and forces him to amend. The writer wryly suggests that subsequent officials in Jerusalem were given the job as a punishment. The oppression of the faithful is described in gruesome detail, especially the tale of the seven brothers and their martyrdom.

probably written by the Covenanters rather than copied from elsewhere, include descriptions of the community and its beliefs, and examples of their own method of expounding scripture. Parts of Jubilees, 1 Enoch, and the Testaments of the Twelve Patriarchs have been found, together with a few scraps of Tobit and Ecclesiasticus. Not all the books are in their familiar form; some differences are due to errors in transmission, others, such as those in the Testament of Naphtali, represent another version of the work. Many fragments of the Zadokite work have been found, which the Covenanters used, together with two similar books generally known as the 'Manual of Discipline' and the 'Rule of the Congregation'. All the regulations are set in the context of the Covenanters' battle against the 'Angel of Darkness'. The 'Children of Light' believed that they were living in the last days. They expected a Messiah 'of Aaron and Israel' and they attached great importance to their priests. The language is often like that of the Fourth Gospel.

In view of the known apocalypses found at Qumran, it is not surprising that their own compositions are similar. Some of the most important scrolls are a small 'Book of Mysteries' describing the future banishment of darkness by light, a description of the 'New Jerusalem' in the manner of Ezekiel, an 'Angelic Liturgy' devoted to the seven archangels and Yahweh's throne chariot, 'Hymns' claiming insight into mysteries and describing the birth pains of God's kingdom, and 'The War of the Sons of Light against the Sons of Darkness'. This war scroll is a strange combination of theological and military preparations for the 'Last Battle'. The struggles of the near future would be of cosmic significance. The defeat of the enemy, 'the Sons of Darkness', would end all evil and establish a kingdom of God. The hopes of the apocalyptists were becoming reality; the birth pangs of the Messianic Age were no figure of speech.

The Covenanters had their own method of expounding scripture. A commentary on Habakkuk is the largest of these works to survive, and shows how all-pervading was the apocalyptic outlook. Just as descriptions of the present were put in the form of pseudonymous prophecies from the past, so genuine prophecy was held to be a 'mystery', whose real interpretation could be seen in present events. These events, broadly speaking, were contemporary with the origins of Christianity. This mass of new evidence has made it necessary to re-examine many ideas; some have been modified, many clarified.

The importance of the non-canonical writings in these new developments means that their relevance to the New Testament may be greater than was once thought possible. They were, after all, preserved by Christian hands. To take up the New Testament after reading the Apocrypha and Pseudepigrapha is to come to it afresh. Matthew seems very different when one has read 1 Enoch, as does the Fourth Gospel after reading parts of the Scrolls. The question of any *direct* relationship with the New Testament, however, is another matter. The Scrolls in fact illustrate how much was held in common by different groups of Jews in the time just before the New Testament; but they illustrate also great differences. For example, the Covenanters made all their members keep the Law very strictly, and awaited a Messiah or Messiahs; the Christian Church believed the authority of the Law had been superseded by the Messiah having already come in Jesus, and they worshipped him in a way the Covenanters would have thought shocking.

The relation of the Scrolls to the Old Testament, on the other hand, is direct. These 'other writings' can only be appreciated in the context of the Judaism whence they came, and are a constant reminder that, as more becomes known of these 'other writings' of the Jewish community, so greater light may be shed on the origins of Christianity, and the extent of its Jewish inheritance be more fully appreciated and understood.

SUGGESTIONS FOR FURTHER READING

E. R. BEVAN *Jerusalem under the High Priests*, London, 1904.

W. R. FARMER *Maccabees, Zealots and Josephus*, New York, 1956.

H. H. ROWLEY *The Relevance of Apocalyptic*, London, 1947.

——'Apocalyptic Literature' – article in *Peake's Commentary on the Bible*, London, 1962.

D. S. RUSSELL *Between the Testaments*, London, 1960

——*The Jews from Alexander to Herod* (New Clarendon Bible, vol. 5), Oxford, 1967.

The Jewish–Alexandrian philosopher Philo, writing in the middle of the same century, and the Jewish historian Josephus at its end, both refer to 'the sacred scriptures' (*Life of Moses* 2: 29, *Antiquities* I, iii, 13); other Jewish descriptions of the same period are 'what is read', 'what is written', and 'the Book'.

From these rather imposing titles we gather that by the second century A.D. the Old Testament was deeply respected; but there is also evidence that this veneration was granted only to a limited number of books – in other words, that there was some sort of a canon of scripture. Rabbinic works of the early Christian era refer to certain books as 'defiling the hands', that is, as being so sacred that to touch them must be followed by ceremonial handwashing to wash away the sacred substance. Josephus in *Against Apion* I: 8 (about A.D. 100), writing to try and show that the historical evidence in the Old Testament is reliable, stresses that the Jews did not have a large number of books which contradicted each other but a limited number which were completely to be trusted. These books (twenty-two according to Jospehus; several of them made up of what we now know as separate works) are the contents of the Hebrew Old Testament, still accepted as canonical by Jews and Christians.

How did this state of affairs come about? There is no record of previous decisions by councils or authorities declaring which works were to be canonical and which were not. The only occasion when something like this could have happened was during the activities associated with Jewish Rabbis at Jamnia (Jabneh) on the coast of Palestine in the last years of the first century A.D. The details are disputed, but it seems that after the fall of Jerusalem to Rome in A.D. 70, permission was given by the Roman authorities for the re-establishment of an assembly of religious teachers at Jamnia. There are Rabbinic records of debates on the authority of certain books, notably Ecclesiastes and the Song of Songs, and although there is no surviving official pronouncement it may well have been that during this troubled period Judaism felt the need to make sure of her heritage in the scriptures, and at the same time to settle the practical question of which books were to be used in worship.

However, what, if anything, happened at Jamnia can only be a matter of conjecture; we are still left with the question of how and when the canon emerged. According to tradition Ezra was responsible for its final compilation; 2 Esdras 14 tells the story (see p. 82). Josephus, although he counts twenty-two books instead of the twenty-four of the Esdras account, also insists that they were completed by the time of Artaxerxes I of Persia (465–424 B.C.) which coincides with Ezra; *Baba Bathra* 14*b*–15*a* (a Jewish work dated about A.D. 180) states that no works in the canon were composed before Moses, and none after Artaxerxes.

This theory about the origin of the canon was accepted, sometimes in modified form, by Christians as late as the eighteenth century. But literary and historical analysis have made it virtually untenable by showing that some books were not written until after Ezra's time, so we are left to try and trace what must in fact have been a long and gradual process of assimilation, acceptance and rejection, knowing that such an attempt is unlikely to end in a tidily documented history. We must also realize that knowing the approximate date of a book's appearance as a complete work does not necessarily mean knowing when it was accepted as authoritative. Obviously a work could not become canonical until it had been written, but there is no evidence that all the Old Testament books were acclaimed as sacred scripture the minute they became known; on the contrary most of them seem to have been in circulation for some time before people finally made up their minds about them. But bearing in mind these difficulties, it is still possible to find evidence of attitudes towards certain books or groups of books at certain times which may help us to form some kind of idea of the way in which the canon had evolved by the time of Josephus.

A good starting place is the Hebrew Old Testament itself, which provides the first clue by the arrangement of its contents. The books fall into three groups: the Law, the Prophets and the Writings; in Hebrew *Torah*, *Nebi'im* and *Kethubim*, the whole still known to the Jews as *Tanak*, an abbreviation from the initial letters. The order of these sections seems roughly to correspond not only with the order of their acceptance but also with the degree of authority accorded them. We will look at the evidence concerning each in turn.

The Law

The Law, or Torah, consists of the first five books of the Old Testament. The word *torah* originally meant oral instruction or direction, often on religious matters; in Hag. 2: 11 the priests are asked to give 'their *ruling*', or torah, on a ritual point. The same word occurs in Ezek. 44: 24, again with reference to the priests: 'when disputes break out, they shall... settle the case according to my *rules*'. It was also used of a definite collection of law which had been written down: Hos. 8: 12, 'countless *rules* in writing'; Josh. 24: 26, 'the book of the *law* of

God'. Eventually, 'Torah' came to be the proper name for the whole Pentateuch, in which the most important legal collections are included. Of course there is a good deal of narrative material as well, and the name equally applies to this. The implication is that not only the actual law codes give guidance; the whole story of God's dealing with Israel provides instruction and direction.

From early times in Israel certain formulae seem to have been recognized as divinely inspired and authoritative; Exod. 20: 1 introduces the Ten Commandments with 'God spoke, and these were his words'; after the giving of the Law on Mount Sinai the people declared, 'We will obey, and do all that the LORD has said' (Exod. 24: 7); and there are references to laws being written down and deliberately preserved. According to Deut. 31: 9, 'Moses wrote down this law and gave it to the priests, the sons of Levi, who carried the Ark of the Covenant of the LORD, and to all the elders of Israel' – see also Josh. 24: 25, 26 and 1 Sam. 10: 25.

Then in 621 B.C. during the cleaning and renovation of the temple at Jerusalem a 'book of the law' was discovered, and read first by the temple authorities and then by king Josiah himself. The story is told in 2 Kings 22 and 23. As a result, a radical religious reformation was initiated; foreign elements were eliminated from the worship of Yahweh, and it was decreed that sacrifice must take place only at the central sanctuary in Jerusalem, and not as previously at local shrines. These and other reforms correspond closely with the standards laid down in Deuteronomy, and it is generally agreed that the book found in the temple was a substantial part of Deuteronomy as we know it. Of course, there must have been subsequent additions and modifications; but in spite of later changes and lapses on the part of the people, the standards of this book survived the exile in Babylon. Some of Nehemiah's reforms in Judaea in the middle of the fifth century B.C. are definitely related to the Deuteronomic law; one such is the exclusion of the Moabites and Ammonites from the community (see Neh. 13: 23 ff. and Deut. 23: 3 ff.).

The story of the discovery of the book in the temple is important, not only because the collection of laws was immediately recognized as inspired, but also because official action was taken by royal command, and because this was more than a superficial clearing up of irregularities – it involved a re-thinking of the nation's whole outlook and behaviour in relation to its God. When the reforms were complete there was a celebration of the Passover (2 Kings 23: 21), setting the seal upon the acceptance of the 'book of the law' as a permanent rule for community life.

About two hundred years later, when many of the people of Judah and Jerusalem had been exiled for generations, and a small and struggling community had returned to Judaea and was trying, under Persian rule, to revive its economic, political and religious life, Ezra came to Jerusalem from Babylon. He was 'a scribe learned in the law of Moses', who 'had devoted himself to the study and observance of the law of the LORD and to teaching statute and ordinance in Israel' (Ezra 7: 6, 10), and he came 'entrusted with the law of (his) God' (Ezra 7: 14), which he was to administer. Neh. 8–10 records that Ezra organized in Jerusalem a public reading and explanation of 'the book of the law', and once more the Law was not only read but acted upon. The Feast of Tabernacles was celebrated – according to Neh. 8: 17 the first proper observance since the days of Joshua.

Here again, we cannot be sure about the exact contents of this book. It may have been another of the strands of tradition which finally made up the Pentateuch – the one known as the Priestly Code, which included most of Leviticus, the laws in later Exodus and in Numbers, and some narrative material, and which is thought to have been completed by the late fifth or early fourth century B.C. Certainly the keeping of the feast is in accordance with the requirements of this tradition (see Neh. 8: 13–18 and Lev. 23: 39–43). Or perhaps the book was the whole Pentateuch; it can be argued that it would be strange if there were a record of the acceptance of Deuteronomy and of the Priestly Code, but none of the acceptance of the Torah as a whole. What does seem clear is that by the time of Nehemiah and Ezra (Nehemiah returned to Jerusalem as governor for the first time in 444 B.C.; Ezra's dates are suggested as 458 B.C. or, more probably, 398 B.C.), not only Deuteronomy but also a further body of law was recognized as the basic standard for worship and conduct in the post-exilic state.

Often cited as evidence regarding the development of the canon is the existence of the Samaritan Pentateuch. The present-day Samaritans, a small community concentrated around Nablus, near the site of biblical Shechem, accept as canonical only the first five books of the Old Testament. Their namesakes of New Testament times adopted the same attitude; surviving Samaritan literature shows that they knew of the existence of the Former Prophets (Joshua, Judges, 1 and 2 Samuel and 1 and 2 Kings) and even of the work of the Chronicler, but denied to them the authority of the Torah, as indeed did many Jews until the Christian era. In addition there were tensions between the Samaritans and their Jewish neighbours; the parable of the Good Samaritan (Luke 10: 25-37) implies that it was a matter for comment when a member of one group went out of his way to help a member of the other.

Obviously at some stage the Samaritans must have become estranged from more orthodox Judaism, taking with them the Pentateuch as their canon of scripture. Suggested dates for the 'Samaritan schism', as it is sometimes called, range from the fifth century B.C. onwards, but it should more probably be seen as a gradual process continuing until the second or first centuries B.C. It seems reasonable to suppose that whenever the breach became open the Torah had already been held in high esteem for some time. So the conclusions that we can draw from the Samaritan canon are limited – namely that the first five books of the Bible were established as authoritative before about the second century B.C.

The place of the Torah at the beginning of the canon indicates not only its comparatively early acceptance, but also its supreme importance. The Pharisees said contemptuously, 'this rabble, which cares nothing for the Law, a curse is on them' (John 7: 49); the Rabbis exhorted, 'make the study of the Law thy special business'; and the Pentateuch retained for the Jews a central position long after the rest of the Hebrew Bible had become canonical. It was the Law as revealed to Moses, and so although in a literary sense Joshua and even some of the later historical books were drawn from the same sources and edited by the same hands, in a canonical sense there is a decisive break after the death of Moses at the end of Deuteronomy. The rest of the scriptures in the main only confirm the Law; they are still often called *kabbalah*, or tradition. Around the Torah grew up the 'unwritten

Law', applying its principles to specific moral, criminal and ritual situations. This oral amplification is called in the New Testament 'tradition' or 'the ancient tradition' (Mark 7: 1-13); later in the Christian era it was written down in the Rabbinic works known as the Mishnah and the Talmud (see p. 171). It is not surprising that sometimes the whole Old Testament is called the Torah; to the Jew, denial of the authority of the Pentateuch would involve rejection of all the rest.

The Prophets

The second part of the Hebrew canon is divided into 'Former' and 'Latter' Prophets. The Former Prophets (Joshua, Judges, 1 and 2 Samuel and 1 and 2 Kings) are books which we might be inclined to regard as history rather than prophecy, although they include the stories of Samuel, Nathan, Elijah, Elisha and others. The Latter Prophets are Isaiah, Jeremiah, Ezekiel and 'the Twelve' minor prophets (see p. 50). 'The Twelve' seem to have counted as one book, perhaps because they fitted conveniently on one scroll.

This division into former and latter, or earlier and later, cannot be traced further back than the eighth century A.D., and is western rather than Hebraic. It may simply have referred to the position of the books in relation to each other, or indicated which were thought to have been written first. But most probably it made a distinction between the historical and the more obviously prophetical material, a distinction which in the Hebrew mind hardly existed. History was concerned with God's dealings with men and with his revelation of himself in events; as well as being a record of the past it was a testimony, example and warning to generations of the future. In that sense it was prophetic, just as the oracle beginning 'These are the words of the LORD' was prophetic.

Although many of the books of prophecy must have been in existence by the time the contents of the Pentateuch were settled (their suggested dates range from about the eighth century B.C. onwards), the 'prophets' section of the canon does not seem to have been established until considerably later. The reason is probably to be found in the very complex way in which the prophetic literature came into being. In the Former Prophets, as in the Pentateuch, different strands of material, written and oral, were gathered together and woven into a narrative which interpreted history and drew conclusions from it in a way reminiscent of the book of Deuteronomy (an example of this outlook is the account in 2 Kings 17 of the fall of the Northern Kingdom – see p. 72). The composition and preservation for posterity of the Latter Prophets is an even more complicated story. No doubt much of the material began as the spoken word, claiming to be a direct message from God, accepted as such by the prophet's disciples, and usually referring to some specific contemporary situation. Isa. 7: 7–9, dealing with the threat to Jerusalem from 'Aram and Israel' (Syria and the Northern Kingdom), is an example:

> This shall not happen now, and never shall,
> for all that the chief city of Aram is Damascus,
> and Rezin is the chief of Damascus;
> within sixty-five years
> Ephraim shall cease to be a nation,
> for all that Samaria is the chief city of Ephraim,
> and Remaliah's son the chief of Samaria.
> Have firm faith, or you will not stand firm.

Such teaching was preserved and transmitted, perhaps by the disciples (Isa. 8: 16, see p. 62), applied to later and more general situations, and at some stage written down. At this point or earlier it might also be seen to have relevance for the future. An instance of the way in which all this could happen is the story in Jer. 36. Jeremiah's spoken prophecies of many years were by divine command written down for the specific purpose of encouraging king Jehoiakim and the people to change their way of life and seek God's forgiveness. After the king, angered by its contents, had destroyed the scroll, Jeremiah added another prophecy to his former words, this time concerning the future consequences of the king's attitude to God's message:

Therefore these are the words of the LORD about Jehoiakim king of Judah: He shall have no one to succeed him on the throne of David, and his dead body shall be exposed to scorching heat by day and frost by night. I will punish him and also his offspring and his courtiers for their wickedness, and I will bring down on them and on the inhabitants of Jerusalem and on the men of Judah all the calamities with which I threatened them, and to which they turned a deaf ear (Jer. 36: 30, 31).

Presumably the new oracle was included and preserved in the rewritten manuscript.

This process of addition, enlargement and re-application might, one would think, have gone on for ever. In fact it did not. Ben Sirach, writing a little after 200 B.C., has a famous passage celebrating Israel's heroes (Ecclus. 44–50). In it he mentions the chief characters of Samuel and Kings, including the prophet Isaiah, and also speaks of Jeremiah, Ezekiel and 'the Twelve', from which it seems clear that the minor prophets were already an established collection. We cannot, of course, tell whether the books known to Ben Sirach were exactly the same as the ones we now know, but we do gather that he knew the later as well as the earlier parts of Isaiah. In Ecclus. 48: 24, 25 he writes of Isaiah:

> With inspired power he saw the future
> and comforted the mourners in Zion.
> He revealed things to come before they happened,
> the secrets of the future to the end of time,

which seems to be a direct reference to Isa. 61: 2:

> to comfort all who mourn,

and to Isa. 42: 9:

> See how the first prophecies have come to pass,
> and now I declare new things.

Later in the century (dates suggested are 132 or 117 B.C.), Ben Sirach's grandson translated Ecclesiasticus from Hebrew into Greek and in his preface referred to his grandfather's study of 'the law, the prophets, and the other writings of our ancestors'. From this it appears that by Ben Sirach's time the three-part canon was in existence and the Law and the Prophets were fixed, although the third group was not yet definitely rounded off, nor had it been given a name of its own.

Ben Sirach himself evidently saw no reason why his own writings should not be set alongside the prophets as inspired:

> As for me...
> I will again pour out doctrine like prophecy
> and bequeath it to future generations (Ecclus. 24: 30, 33),

but this did not happen. No further books were added to the second section of the canon: Daniel (thought to have been written between 168 and 165 B.C.) never found a permanent place, and the Qumran community's collection of sacred writings apparently does not include it among the Prophets.

The tacit agreement to call a halt at this particular juncture is probably bound up with what was happening to prophecy in general. By 200 B.C. or thereabouts it had fallen into disrepute: the direct voice of God was seldom heard. More than five hundred years earlier the prophet Amos had given warning:

> The time is coming, says the Lord GOD,
> when I will send famine on the land,
> not hunger for bread or thirst for water,
> but for hearing the word of the LORD (Amos 8: 11).

Now it looked as if this was happening. Apocalyptic was gaining in reputation; late additions to the prophets such as Hab. 3 and Zech. 9–14 marked the transition. Zech. 13: 3 ff. bitterly describes the state of things:

Thereafter, if a man continues to prophesy, his parents, his own father and mother, will say to him, 'You shall live no longer, for you have spoken falsely in the name of the LORD.' His own father and mother will pierce him through because he has prophesied. On that day every prophet shall be ashamed of his vision when he prophesies, nor shall he wear a robe of coarse hair in order to deceive. He will say, 'I am no prophet, I am a tiller of the soil who has been schooled in lust from boyhood.'

The same situation is reflected in 1 Maccabees. When Judas Maccabaeus cleansed the desecrated temple in 165 B.C., the altar of burnt offering, defiled by the Gentiles, was dismantled and its stones stored away 'until a prophet should arise who could be consulted about them' (1 Macc. 4: 46), the inference being that no such prophet could be found at the time. After the death of Judas, 'It was a time of great affliction for Israel, worse than any since the day when prophets ceased to appear among them' (1 Macc. 9: 27); some years later Simon Maccabaeus was made leader and high priest 'in perpetuity until a true prophet should appear' (1 Macc. 14: 41). This hope is echoed in the New Testament. The priests and Levites said to John the Baptist, 'Are you the prophet we await?' (John 1: 21). Asked by Jesus, 'Who do men say I am?', his disciples answered, 'Some say John the Baptist, others Elijah, others one of the prophets' (Mark 8: 28).

But no such prophet materialized. Instead, there was increasing dependence on exegesis and application of earlier prophecy (the Habakkuk Commentary is one such example – see pp. 103, 173). Although there may have been additions to individual books, the Former and Latter Prophets were to comprise the whole of the second section of the canon; future writings were to find a home within its third section.

The Writings

The Hebrew *Kethubim* means '(things) written'; sometimes the Greek *Hagiographa*, meaning 'sacred writings', is used. It is not certain whether these rather vague titles, and the 'other writings' of the preface to Ecclesiasticus, indicate some difference in importance between these books and the rest of the canon, but it is a fact that whereas the Torah and the Prophets were read regularly in the synagogue, of the Hagiographa only the Psalms found a place in the service.

The process by which these works came to be accepted as canonical is even more elusive and difficult to trace than the story of the first two sections of the canon. The Writings vary widely in character and contents, and for this reason no doubt they circulated independently before they were absorbed into the canon. In the Hebrew Old Testament similar kinds of books are grouped together; first, three books of poetry (Psalms, Proverbs and Job), then the 'Five Rolls' (the Song of Songs, Ruth, Lamentations, Ecclesiastes and Esther), each of which has at least since the Middle Ages been read at one of the major Jewish festivals. Next comes Daniel, which might claim to be part prophetic, part apocalyptic, and finally the work of the editor known as the Chronicler – Ezra–Nehemiah and 1 and 2 Chronicles. So the books of the complete Hebrew canon are

the Torah – Genesis   Numbers
Exodus   Deuteronomy
Leviticus

then

the Prophets – Joshua
Judges
1 and 2 Samuel   } the 'Former Prophets'
1 and 2 Kings
Isaiah
Jeremiah
Ezekiel   } the 'Latter Prophets'
'The Twelve'

and finally

the Writings – Psalms   Ecclesiastes
Proverbs   Esther
Job   Daniel
Song of Songs   Ezra
Ruth   Nehemiah
Lamentations   1 and 2 Chronicles.

Lacking the obvious authority of the Torah and the Prophets, how did these books get into the canon at all? Some had traditional connections with great names of the past; Lamentations with Jeremiah, the Psalms with David, and Proverbs, Ecclesiastes and the Song of Songs with Solomon. Ben Sirach says that David

> . . . sang hymns of praise,
> to show his love for his Maker (Ecclus. 47: 8),

and refers to the 'proverbs and riddles' of Solomon (Ecclus. 47: 15). Even apart from these associations, in Israel songs and wisdom poetry were among the types of literature which were accorded a high degree of inspiration, which would account for the inclusion of Job as well as of the other books of poetry and wisdom. Then the associations of the 'Five Rolls' with the festivals may stretch a good deal further back than we know, especially that of Esther with the Feast of Purim, the origin of which is actually explained in Esther 9: 23–8. Daniel, though not given a permanent place among the Prophets, nevertheless seems always to have been accorded a good deal of the respect usually reserved for books of prophecy, and the work of the Chronicler deals with history, law and worship in a way which would particularly commend itself to the Jews in the centuries after the exile, as they struggled hard to preserve their moral and religious independence against successive occupying powers. Of course, much of this can only be surmise, but it may give some idea of the grounds on which this part of the canon gradually came to be accepted.

What of the way in which it was collected and selected? Ben Sirach mentions Nehemiah (Ecclus. 49: 13), and as we have seen attributes certain works to David and Solomon; his grandson's reference to 'other writings' and 'the rest of the writings' does not mention any by name. 1 Maccabees (written towards the end of the reign of John Hyrcanus in 104 B.C. – see p. 100), describing a particularly unpleasant mass arrest and execution during Judas' rebellion, comments:

as Scripture says:
'The bodies of thy saints were scattered,
their blood was shed round Jerusalem,
and there was none to bury them' (1 Macc. 7: 17),

which seems to be a fairly straight quotation from Ps. 79: 2, 3:

They have thrown out the dead bodies of thy servants
to feed the birds of the air...
Their blood is spilled all round Jerusalem like water,
and there they lie unburied.

2 Maccabees, compiled and edited by an Alexandrian author in mid-first century B.C. (see pp. 100,101), is familiar with stories of Nehemiah and Esther and knows of the custom of singing psalms (though what these psalms were we do not know). Perhaps more significant is the reference to the actual collecting of books together; 2 Macc. 2: 13–15 records: 'Just as Nehemiah collected the chronicles of the kings, the writings of prophets, the works of David, and royal letters about sacred offerings, to found his library, so Judas also has collected all the books that had been scattered as a result of our recent conflict.' Philo, writing in *De Vita Contempliva*, in about A.D. 40, quotes from all the Writings except Daniel, Chronicles and the 'Five Rolls', and describes the Therapeutae, a contemporary religious order, as taking into their cells 'only laws and words prophesied by prophets, and psalms, and

the other writings by which knowledge and piety may be increased and perfected'.

All this adds up to the fact that in Jewish literature of the last two centuries B.C. and the first century of the Christian era there are a number of references to a (probably growing) collection of sacred books other than the Law and the Prophets, and some of them are quoted as scripture. But we cannot tell how far these works correspond to the Hagiographa as we know it, nor is there any evidence that at this stage the apocryphal books were held in any less esteem.

In the New Testament there is again evidence of the threefold canon; Luke 24: 44 speaks of 'the Law of Moses and...the prophets and psalms', probably identifying the Hagiographa by the name of its most notable book. In Luke 11: 50, 51 Jesus is recorded as saying 'this generation will have to answer for the blood of all the prophets shed since the foundation of the world; from the blood of Abel to the blood of Zechariah who perished between the altar and the sanctuary'. The 'blood of Abel' refers of course to the first murder in the Old Testament (Gen. 4: 1–16); the 'blood of Zechariah' has been interpreted as a reference to the last murder in the Hebrew canon, that of Zechariah son of Jehoiada (Matt. 23: 35 has 'Zechariah son of Berachiah', perhaps in confusion with the Old Testament 'writing' prophet), who pronounced the judgement of God upon the people and was stoned to death by them (2 Chron. 24: 20–2). If this were so, these verses in Luke and Matthew would be tantamount to saying 'from one end of the scriptures to the other', and would be strong evidence that the limits of the canon were effectively fixed by the time the Gospels were written. This may well have been true, but we cannot cite the saying with any certainty, since there is an alternative possibility that the reference may be to a much later Zechariah, also murdered in the temple. Another difficulty is that this argument assumes that the writer of the first Gospel knew a number of Old Testament books published together in a fixed order with Chronicles at the end, whereas it is far more likely that at this stage there were individual scrolls, the order of which could be changed. So the reference to Chronicles by no means implies that it was the last book of the canon.

As to content, the New Testament quotes from or refers to every book in the Old Testament except Ecclesiastes, Esther and the Song of Songs. This omission may have been chance, or it may have reflected the fact that these books were still struggling for recognition at the time of Jamnia. The scriptures are referred to as inspired (2 Tim. 3: 16, 'Every inspired scripture has its use for teaching the truth and refuting error, or for reformation of manners and discipline in right living'), and as authoritative (Matt. 21: 42, 'Have you never read in the scriptures: "The stone which the builders rejected has become the main corner-stone"... *Therefore*, I tell you, the kingdom of God will be taken away from you, and given to a nation that yields the proper fruit'). Indeed, their authority is such that it is enough to say 'Scripture says' (Matt. 4: 4, 6, 10; Gal. 3: 13). On the other hand the text, though sacred, is by no means sacrosanct. Quotations are run together (Matt. 3: 17, 'This is my Son, my Beloved, on whom my favour rests', seems to be a conflation of Ps. 2: 7, 'You are my son', and Isa. 42: 1, 'My chosen one in whom I delight'), and passages are quoted as scripture yet cannot be traced in the Old Testament (two examples are Matt. 2: 23,

'This was to fulfil the words spoken through the prophets: "He shall be called a Nazarene"', and Jas. 4: 5, 'Or
do you suppose that Scripture has no meaning when it
says that the spirit which God implanted in man turns
towards envious desires?').

There are references to books outside the Hebrew
canon; not only to the apocryphal books which were
included in the Septuagint (Luke 11: 49, 'The Wisdom of
God said' may simply mean 'God in his wisdom said',
but has also been interpreted as citing the Wisdom of
Solomon from the Apocrypha), but also to the Pseudepigrapha (Jude 9 refers to the story told in the Assumption
of Moses; Jude 14 quotes from Enoch 1: 9 in the passage
beginning, 'I saw the Lord come with his myriads of
angels, to bring all men to judgement'). As far as we can
tell, for the early Christian as for the Jew there was a
definite body of scripture regarded as authoritative, but
its limits were as yet less sharply defined than those of the
sacred books of Judaism.

The completion of the canon

And so we come back to Jamnia, and to Josephus and his
twenty-two books. Even now, by no means everything
was settled once and for all with regard to content,
number or arrangement. Ecclesiastes and the Song of
Songs continued to be regarded as doubtful, although
according to the Mishnah (*Yadaim* iii) they were the
subject of the decision at Jamnia that 'the Song of Songs
and Ecclesiastes both defile the hands'. As late as the
fourth century A.D., Esther was omitted by the Christian
writer Athanasius from the Old Testament proper and
included among apocryphal works as being edifying but
not authoritative. Ruth, Proverbs and Ezekiel also had

their critics from time to time, and the placing of Chronicles after Ezra–Nehemiah may indicate that it was later in finding an assured place in the canon even though the story which it tells is earlier. Apocryphal books were excluded by the Rabbis (no doubt the predilection of the Christian Church for the Septuagint which included them had a good deal to do with their rejection) but they may from time to time have been considered. Akiba (see p. 75) writes so violently against Ecclesiasticus that one wonders whether in his day it was being used as scripture, and Origen, the Christian Father of the third century A.D., says that Baruch was currently received in some Rabbinic circles. But these were on the whole minor variations. The main form and contents of the Hebrew canon were decided by A.D. 100.

As to the numbering of the books, we count thirty-nine to the Old Testament, Josephus counts twenty-two as do Origen and Jerome, and 2 Esdras and *Baba Bathra* have twenty-four. How can we reconcile these figures? Our thirty-nine is reduced to twenty-two if the books of the Pentateuch remain unchanged but Judges and Ruth are counted as one, as are 1 and 2 Samuel, 1 and 2 Kings, 1 and 2 Chronicles, Ezra–Nehemiah, Jeremiah–Lamentations, and 'the Twelve'. The twenty-two becomes twenty-four if we separate Judges from Ruth and Jeremiah from Lamentations. Peoples of the ancient world often had a great interest in number-symbolism, and it may be that Josephus' total of twenty-two books was consciously related to the number of letters in the Hebrew alphabet, whilst the twenty-four of 2 Esdras' and *Baba Bathra*'s reckoning represented twice the number of the Hebrew tribes. The seventy 'secret' books dictated by Ezra (see p. 82) may also represent a sacred number.

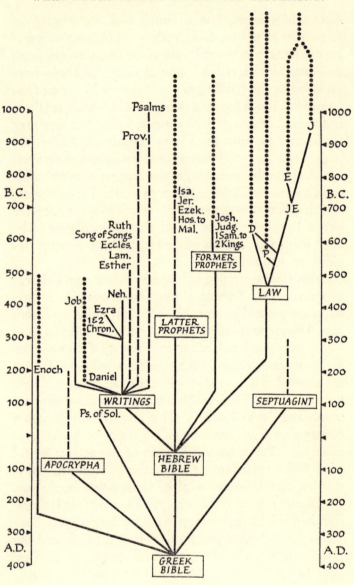

Seven and its multiples were accorded special significance in Egyptian, Assyrian and Persian religions (perhaps associated with the seven days of the week, perhaps with the worship of the seven heavenly bodies – sun, moon, and five planets) and appear frequently in connection with ritual in the Old Testament.

Although the grouping of the canon in three sections was fixed at an early stage, the arrangement and allocation of the Prophets and the Hagiographa varied considerably between versions used by the Jews during the early Christian era (the Torah seems to have remained constant, probably because its order follows from the nature of the books). It is true that the Former Prophets, apart from the inclusion or non-inclusion of Ruth with Judges, did not vary; they accord with the sequence of events. But among the Latter Prophets *Baba Bathra* places Isaiah after Jeremiah and Ezekiel but before 'the Twelve', perhaps acknowledging that Isaiah as a whole is a later book than either Jeremiah or Ezekiel.

The Writings seem to have been arranged and rearranged. Sometimes Psalms, Proverbs and Job (or

---

4. The growth of the Old Testament (from *Old Testament Illustrations*, by C. M. Jones). This diagram is an attempt to show how the Old Testament came into being. A dotted line (....) represents the period during which the material was passed on by word of mouth from one generation to the next; a broken line (– – – –) represents the period during which this oral material was put into writing; and a full line (——) represents the period during which this written material was passed on from one generation to the next. The oral period goes back much further than can be shown on the diagram, probably to a time not much later than the settlement of the Hebrews in Canaan after the exodus.

Psalms, Job and Proverbs) would be at the beginning and Ezra–Nehemiah and Chronicles at the end; in other versions Chronicles would be placed at the beginning. The grouping of the 'Five Rolls' together appears regularly only from the sixth century A.D. onwards; the order Song of Songs–Ruth–Lamentations–Ecclesiastes–Esther, which corresponds to the order in the calendar of the feasts during which they are used (Passover, Pentecost, the anniversary of the destruction of Jerusalem in 586 B.C., Tabernacles and Purim), first became established in the twelfth century A.D.

Josephus had his own ideas as to what constituted the Prophets and the Writings; in his threefold canon he lists thirteen books compiled by the prophets who followed Moses, and four books of hymns and precepts. His prophetic books are Joshua, Judges–Ruth, Samuel, Kings, Isaiah, Jeremiah–Lamentations, Ezekiel, 'the Twelve', Job, Daniel, Esther, Ezra–Nehemiah and Chronicles. The 'hymns and precepts' are Psalms, Proverbs, Song of Songs and Ecclesiastes – that is, David's Psalter and the three works popularly connected with Solomon.

The Old Testament in English

So much for the Hebrew Old Testament as it emerged and as we have it today. When, however, we compare it with the Old Testament in English we are left with two further questions: first, why is the English Bible arranged differently, and secondly, why are books of the Apocrypha included in some versions and not in others?

For the answers we must go back to the Septuagint, which was arranged not in three groups roughly representing the stages of canonization but according to subject-matter; first Law (the Torah as always being of primary importance), then history, then poetry, and finally prophecy. This order has been described as educational in intent; it traces the progression of divine revelation first in the events of the past, then in the poetic books with their relevance to their own times, and finally in prophecy, which as well as its contemporary message was directed towards the future. The English versions, even where they have the same contents as the Hebrew canon, have adhered to the arrangement of the Septuagint. So we have Ezra–Nehemiah and Chronicles with the history books, Daniel included with the prophets, and the 'Five Rolls' dispersed among the historical, poetic and prophetic sections.

As regards the inclusion of Apocryphal books in some English versions, the Douay version of 1609, Knox's translation of 1949 and the Jerusalem Bible (English version dated 1966), all of them Roman Catholic translations, add to the Hebrew canon Tobit, Judith, 1 and 2 Maccabees, certain extensions of the book of Daniel (the Song of the Three, Daniel and Susanna, and Daniel, Bel, and the Snake), the Wisdom of Solomon, Ecclesiasticus and Baruch. These are included not as an appendix but in their places alongside the historical, prophetic and wisdom literature. Although there are a great many variations in Septuagint manuscripts, most of them include these apocryphal books, and sometimes others such as 1 and 2 Esdras and 3 and 4 Maccabees. Because of these additions the term 'Alexandrian canon' (see p. 76) is often used, though in fact it is not really a canon, since its contents were always variable and never finally fixed. The early Christian Church, as we have seen, used this Greek Bible with its wider selection of books, and continued to do so in spite of the Vulgate (see pp. 151-4), Jerome's great translation which he based in the first place on the Hebrew Old Testament, only including the Apocryphal books under protest. In 1546 the Council of Trent affirmed the 'deutero-canonicity' of the Apocrypha, and this was endorsed by the Vatican Council of 1870. Strictly speaking, 'deutero-canonicity' means a secondary type of canonicity, but in fact the Apocryphal books have been accepted by the Roman Catholic Church as in effect fully canonical. The preface to the 1899 edition of the Douay version makes the position clear: 'the Old Testament containing as it does all embraced in the Septuagint, is not only genuine and authentic, but having the approbation of our Saviour and Apostles...has superadded to it the supreme character of divine inspiration, which it possesses to the exclusion of all other versions'.

Meanwhile, following the Reformation, the Protestant Churches took to producing translations which contained only the books of the Hebrew canon; Luther included the Apocrypha in his Bible but explained that it was edifying rather than authoritative; Calvin excluded it altogether. The first edition of the Authorized Version, published in 1611, had the Apocrypha bound between the two Testaments, but later it came to be omitted from the majority of bibles produced. Article six of the Thirty-nine articles of Religion states the Anglican position: 'And the other books (as Jerome saith) the Church doth read for example of life and instruction of manners; but yet doth it not apply them to establish any doctrine'; the Westminster Confession (representing the Presbyterian tradition) goes further and lays down that 'not being of divine inspiration' they 'are of no authority in the Church of God', but merely the same as 'other human writings'.

This divergence between the attitudes of Christian communions towards the Apocrypha was for a long time a hindrance to the acceptance of a common Bible translation by Roman Catholics and the various Protestant bodies. The N.E.B. follows the practice of the first Authorized Version; the Apocrypha is placed at the end of the Old Testament, but after the list of the sponsoring Churches the following note is added: 'The publication of the books of the Apocrypha in this translation prepared under the auspices of the Joint Committee on the New Translation of the Bible does not imply that the bodies represented on the Joint Committee hold a common opinion upon the canonical status of these books.'

More will be said in the last chapter about the varying attitudes of present-day Jews and Christians to the Old Testament books. But any understanding of the terms 'canon' or 'canonical' or 'canonicity' cannot be separated from the view which is taken of biblical authority. If this is definite and rigid, then a strict definition of the canon follows; if it is broader and looser, there can be a 'blurring at the edges' of the canon.

SUGGESTIONS FOR FURTHER READING

P. R. Ackroyd and C. F. Evans (eds.) *The Cambridge History of the Bible* (vol. I, Chapter III (6)). Article by G. W. Anderson on 'Canonical and Non-canonical', Cambridge, 1970.

D. R. Ap-Thomas *A Primer of Old Testament Criticism*, Oxford, 1965.

E. E. FLACK, B. M. METZGER *et al.* *The Text, Canon, and Principal Versions of the Bible*, Ann Arbor, 1956.

GEOFFREY HUNT *About the New English Bible*, Cambridge, 1970.

L. M. MARGOLIS *The Hebrew Scriptures in the Making*, Philadelphia, 1922.

H. H. ROWLEY *The Growth of the Old Testament*, London, 1950.

5

FROM THE ANCIENT LANGUAGES TO THE NEW ENGLISH BIBLE

Introduction

'So what is the Bible?' Clearly we cannot give an exhaustive answer by merely pointing to an actual copy of the bible which may happen to be on our bookshelf and saying, 'That is.' It would be no less absurd to point to even every English version of the bible, for they are but translations of older non-English bibles. And if we tried to point to those older non-English bibles, again we should be in difficulties, because some English bibles are translations of the Latin bible, and some of a mixture of the Hebrew and the Greek bibles.

The proper answer to the question, 'What is the Bible?', is that there is no such thing as THE BIBLE. Rather there are many bibles, and they are often very different from each other. All bibles are bibles of particular nations, or else they are the bibles of particular international groups who profess the same religion. The bible of the Jews has become part of the bigger bible of the Christians; it is called by the latter the Old Testament, and by the former, for whom it is the *whole* bible, *Miqra* (the Reading) or *Torah* (the Law; the full title is 'The Law, the Prophets and the Writings', see p. 108). The bible of Roman Catholics is traditionally bigger than the bible of Protestants (pp. 129–30). The Old Testament in Greek was originally the bible of Jews in Egypt (pp. 75, 147) and became part of the bible of the majority of early Christians, whereas the bible in

Latin was never a bible of the Jews but only of the Western Church.

Granted then that there are in fact many bibles, does there remain any virtue in talking about THE BIBLE? The answer is decidedly 'Yes', provided that we think of it as a continuing *tradition*, handed down in various cultures and languages, in speech and in writing, from people to people, from country to country; a tradition which manifests itself in various particular biblical versions and editions. To give an account of the transmission of the Old Testament part of this *tradition* and of its particular manifestations in various languages and at various dates is the purpose of this chapter.

The Hebrew tradition

The Old Testament is part of the Christian bible that has come down the ages to us. Since most of the earliest Christians spoke Greek and received their faith through the medium of that language (for the New Testament is written in Greek), the Old Testament which formed so important a part of their faith was also received and transmitted by them in Greek. We may say, then, that the earliest Old Testament of the Christian tradition was a Greek Old Testament. However, what the Christians call the Old Testament is almost exactly the same as what the Jews call the Law (or the Reading). Since Judaism antedates Christianity, the Jewish (Hebrew) bible (i.e. the Law) preserves a tradition which goes back further into the past than that preserved by the Christian (Greek) Old Testament. Further, since the persons who feature in the Old Testament itself spoke Hebrew and not Greek, it is in the Hebrew tradition that we may expect to come closest to accurate records of their words and actions.

The Hebrew (or Massoretic) Text

Modern printed editions of the Hebrew bible depend upon manuscripts of the ninth and tenth centuries A.D., only those of the tenth century containing all the Old Testament. These manuscripts are the earliest written manifestation of the Hebrew bible; that is to say, together they constitute the earliest *official, complete* Hebrew bible which we possess; they are the earliest written sources for the tradition which the Jews in general regard as their bible. The written tradition or text to which these manuscripts witness is named by scholars the Massoretic (Hebrew = 'traditional') or Received Text. If the reader will recall that the historical events of the exodus are usually dated about the thirteenth century B.C., and that the Patriarchs may belong to about the eighteenth century B.C., it will be readily understood that the written manuscripts of the Hebrew bible which we actually possess do not go back relatively very far. Fortunately, however, various other pieces of evidence enable us to trace back further the written tradition or text, and these will be discussed below. The earliest official Hebrew bible is called the Massoretic Text because it is the end-product, of the work of the Massoretes, a body of Jewish scholars who worked in Palestine and Babylonia between the sixth and tenth centuries A.D. Faced with a variety of differing manuscripts, they sought to make them all conform to the ideal of a single, official Jewish bible which, so far as it was possible, could be read and understood in the same way by all Jews, and to banish from the tradition all manuscripts which did not conform to their standard. One of the most important reasons which impelled them to try to achieve this ideal was that many Jews had already become unfamiliar with the Hebrew language; the Massoretes sought, therefore, an artificial scheme by which to make it easier for Jews to understand Hebrew, and for it to be read in the same way. To explain what this means it is necessary to consider the nature and history of the Hebrew language.

The Hebrew language

The language spoken by the people who feature in the Old Testament is described by the Old Testament itself (Isa. 19: 18, 2 Kings 18: 26, and Neh. 13: 24) as 'the language of Canaan' or 'the language of the Jews'. (N.E.B. in 2 Kings 18: 26 uses the term 'Hebrew' because it is familiar, though a literal translation would be 'Jewish' or 'the language of the Jews'.) Apart from its preservation in the Massoretic Text, it is known to us by a small number of inscriptions on rock or pottery which have survived to the present day. From such evidence we are able to state that the term Hebrew covers a number of very closely related dialects spoken in ancient Palestine. These dialects are part of a family of languages commonly called Semitic (after Shem, mentioned in Gen. 10: 21 ff., the ancestor of the Semitic ethnic group), just as the Italian, Spanish and French family are called Latin languages. The most important languages of the Semitic family, other than Hebrew, are Akkadian (ancient Babylonian and Assyrian), Ugaritic, Arabic, Ethiopic, Punic, Aramaic and Syriac. Of these Arabic and Ethiopic (Amharic) are still spoken today; Syriac is spoken by a small group of Syrian Orthodox Christians in the Near East; Hebrew has been resurrected as the language of the modern State of Israel, though in its present form it has imported much from Western languages.

So alike are Semitic languages in grammatical struc-
ture and vocabulary that scholars believe that they are
descended from a common parent-language, now lost,
which they call Proto-Semitic, spoken by the earliest
Semites before they emigrated in successive waves from
Arabia some time just before 3000 B.C. It is generally
held that Arabic preserves rather more primitive Semitic
elements than do other languages of the family, because it
did not become a literary language until the time of
Mohammed (seventh century A.D.), and had previously
remained free from influence in the relatively isolated
Arabian peninsula.

One of the characteristics which the Semitic languages
share and which enable them to be identified as such is
that most words are formed from triliteral 'roots' to
which other elements are added. For example, *KTB* in
Hebrew and Arabic denotes *he wrote*, *yKTB* denotes *he
will write*. In Hebrew a prefixed *m* gives us a word for a
letter (*miKTaB*). In Arabic the word for a *book* is *KiTaB*,
and in Syriac it is *KTaBa*. Some of the triliteral roots
appear in all the languages of the family: *BYT* denoting
house is pronounced *bitu* in Akkadian, *bayith* or *beyth* in
Hebrew (cp. Beth-lehem, Beth-el, etc.), *baytha* in Aramaic and Syriac, *baytu* in Arabic, and *beth* in Ethiopic.
Not that all roots occur in all the languages; *JLS* denotes
he sat in Arabic whereas Hebrew uses *YSHB*; but the
fact that some words occur in a number of Semitic
languages is of the highest importance to modern scholars
as they seek to understand and translate the Old Testament, and we shall return to this matter later in the
chapter.

Semites, then, emigrating from Arabia in successive
waves, populated Mesopotamia, Syria and Palestine, and

mixed with already existing Semitic and non-Semitic cultures. Israelites in Palestine were of such mixed ancestry as the Old Testament itself declares (the word to Jerusalem in Ezek. 16: 3 is, 'Canaan is the land of your ancestry and there you were born; an Amorite was your father and a Hittite your mother' – see also Gen. 10: 31, Deut. 26: 5), and the Hebrew language accurately reflects this. The phenomenon may be illustrated in the English language, for here, too, there are words of foreign origin such as abbatoir, alcohol, blitz, and synonyms like begin/commence, letter/epistle, end/conclusion, which reflect the origins and history of English, as well as the influences upon the people who speak it.

The Israelites, coming to Palestine in the second half of the second millennium B.C. and speaking a North-West Semitic dialect, mixed with Canaanites. The Canaanite language was itself the result of previous ethnic and linguistic fusion (see p. 26), one of the most important of the elements in which was Babylonian with its cuneiform (wedge-like) writing, which was used as the international military and commerical language from roughly 1900 B.C. to 1300 B.C. The fusion of these elements (Canaanite and the dialect of the invading Israelites) gave rise to the Hebrew of Old Testament times. This language clearly shows its mixed origin; just as *end* in English derives from an Anglo-Saxon source, while *conclude* derives from a Latin source, so one word for *I* in Hebrew (*ani*) comes from an Aramaic/Arabic source (Arabic *ana*) while another (*anoki*) comes from a Babylonian form (*anaku*).

The cuneiform writing of the Babylonians was syllabic rather than alphabetic; that is to say, its signs denoted syllables rather than letters. It was by this system that the

Canaanites wrote their language until the development of alphabetic writing began in Palestine from about 1500 B.C. The alphabet which was developed and which thereafter is characteristic of the writing of all Semitic languages (except Akkadian and Ethiopic) is solely consonantal. In order to illustrate this we may consider a simple English sentence; thus, *the cat was on the mat* written in the consonantal Semitic way would appear as *th ct ws n th mt*. Semitic alphabets imply the notion that speech, when written down, is reducible to consonants, and, indeed, this is facilitated by the triliteral basis of most words. Further, there is reason to suppose that there were only three vowels (a, i, u) in early Semitic speech (including Canaanite/Hebrew), so that difficulties in pronunciation may not have been as great as we might suppose. In later times, however, when people had lost the knowledge of what vowels were intended with the various combinations of consonants, considerable problems arose.

The actual alphabet which emerged in Palestine and surrounding regions is preserved in inscriptions from soon after 1000 B.C., and is known to us as the Phoenician alphabet (because the Phoenicians, ethnically the same as the Canaanites, were responsible for its export), or, alternatively, as the Old Hebrew alphabet (see table on p. 140). With this alphabet, we may be sure, most parts of the Old Testament were first written and transmitted.

Aramaic

Hebrew is not the only language of the Massoretic Text. Certain parts (Ezra 4: 8 – 6: 18, 7: 12–26, Jer. 10: 11 and Dan. 2: 4 – 7: 28) are written in Aramaic. This language was widely diffused in northern Palestine and Syria (called Aram in the Old Testament) from about the

Name	Phonetic equivalent of Semitic letter	Square Hebrew	Samaritan	Phoenician/ Old Hebrew	transition	Classical Greek	transition	Latin
Aleph	'	א	ࠀ	𐤀	ᗡ	A		A
Bêth	b	ב	ࠁ	𐤁	𐌂	B		B
Gimel	g	ג	ࠂ	𐤂	𐌂	Γ		C
Daleth	d	ד	ࠃ	𐤃		Δ	Δ	D
Hê	h	ה	ࠄ	𐤄				
Waw	w	ו	ࠅ	𐤅		Y		Y
Zayin	z	ז	ࠆ	𐤆		I		Z
Ḥêth	ḥ	ח	ࠇ	𐤇		H		H
Têth	ṭ	ט	ࠈ	𐤈		Θ		
Yôdh	y	י	ࠉ	𐤉		I		I
Kaph	k	כ	ࠊ	𐤊	𐌊	K		K
Lāmedh	l	ל	ࠋ	𐤋	𐌋	Λ	ς	L
Mêm	m	מ	ࠌ	𐤌		M		M
Nun	n	נ	ࠍ	𐤍	𐌍	N		N
Sāmeḥ	s	ס	ࠎ	𐤎		Ξ		
'Ayin	'	ע	ࠏ	𐤏		O		O
Pê	p	פ	ࠐ	𐤐	𐌐	Π	𐌓	P
Tsadhê	ts	צ	ࠑ	𐤑				
Qôph	q	ק	ࠒ	𐤒	Φ		Q	Q
Rêsh	r	ר	ࠓ	𐤓		P	R	R
Sîn/Shîn	s (sh)	שׁ	ࠔ	𐤔	𐌔	Σ		S
Taw	t (th)	ת	ࠕ	𐤕		T		T

5. Table of alphabets

The main column shows the Phoenician/Old Hebrew alphabet with (left and right respectively) its development into the Samaritan and the Aramaic (Square Hebrew) scripts, and also into the Latin script by way of the Greek.

tenth century B.C. Like Hebrew it has survived in a few inscriptions from as early as the ninth century B.C., and its script was, at that time, very similar to the Phoenician. From 2 Kings 18: 26 we learn that it was already used in Judah as a diplomatic language, and by the time of the Persian empire, Aramaic had become the official international language of the western provinces of that empire (thus, within the Old Testament Ezra quotes 'official'

NOTE IN EXPLANATION OF THE TABLE OF ALPHABETS

All alphabetic scripts are derived from the Phoenician/Old Hebrew script. The alphabetic Phoenician script is thought to have been derived from Egyptian Hieroglyphic (picture) writing, which gave rise to the invention of the acrophonic principle: every sound was represented by the picture of a particular word which had that sound as an initial characteristic. We may illustrate by supposing that the word *bed* was the word chosen to characterize the sound b, *apple* for the sound a, and *door* for the sound d. So, to write the word *bad* acrophonically, the symbols must be drawn thus: ⊢ ⚬ ⊡. This acrophonic principle underlies the Phoenician alphabet, whose signs are simplifications of the older picture-symbols. *Aleph* (called in Greek *Alpha*) (a) means an ox, and an original drawing of an ox('s head) is modified to ⊀. *Beth* (b) means house, drawn ⊡, thence formalized into ভ in the Phoenician script, and ultimately turned round and closed up into our B. *Mem* (m) means water, and the representation of its ripple ⩘ can still be seen in all symbols for M, including our own.

The word *alphabet* in English is derived, therefore, as is our whole writing system, from the Phoenician/Old Hebrew invention. Over the centuries, however, various modifications have taken place; for example, the sign representing the sound g in Hebrew and Greek is used to represent the k sound in Latin, and becomes Latin (and English) c.

Persian decrees in Aramaic). As the use of Aramaic increased, Hebrew tended to decline except as a language of the cultured and learned. By Nehemiah's time (Neh. 13: 24), Hebrew was already declining in popular circles, and this is why the book of Daniel, intended as a popular work, has a large section in Aramaic (the book is usually dated about 168–165 B.C.). By the time of Christ, Aramaic was much the most widely spoken language of Palestine, though documents such as the Dead Sea Scrolls, as well as the Massoretic Text itself, are an indication of the preservation of Hebrew among the learned and in synagogue worship. As we have indicated above, Aramaic and Hebrew are very closely related, so much so that scholars still dispute whether single Semitic words quoted in the New Testament (for instance, *Ephphatha* in Mark 7: 34) are Hebrew or Aramaic; indeed, when the New Testament speaks of 'Hebrew' it is not always clear whether Hebrew or Aramaic is intended.

One of the most influential legacies of Aramaic is its script. Although descended from the Phoenician script, its development was different from that of the Old Hebrew, and by about the third century B.C. it had assumed a square form which was adopted and used from about 200 B.C. by the Jews to write both Aramaic and Hebrew. It is this Aramaic or 'Square Hebrew' script which thereafter prevailed in Judaism, and with it subsequently the Text has always been written and transmitted. The appearance of this script may be illustrated by the reproduction of the name Solomon, pronounced in Hebrew *Shlomo*: שלמה, and the name Abraham, pronounced *Avrāhām*: אַבְרָהָם. ('Solomon' has been printed without pointing (vowels) and 'Abraham' with it so that the reader may gain some impression of its appearance.)

Massoretic pointing

Having looked at the Hebrew and Aramaic languages and the consonantal character of their scripts, it is now possible to describe the Massoretic Text more fully. It consists of a written consonantal text together with precise instructions as to how it should be read. These instructions are in the form of a series of dots and dashes placed by the Massoretes under, over, or within the consonantal letters. (The dots and dashes are called 'points', and a text which includes both consonants and pointing is called a 'pointed text'.) The effect of this process may, perhaps, best be seen by returning to the English analogy: the reading of the consonantal phrase *th ct ws n th mt* is fixed by pointing, thus: th^e c^at w^as ^on th^e m^at. It will be seen that, without such pointing, the phrase might have been read, for example, as *the coat was on the mat* or as *the cat was in the moat*.

Not only did Massoretic pointing fix the reading of the text in the way that the Massoretes deemed to be correct, it also preserved traditional Jewish interpretations and even corrections of the consonantal text: thus, the name of God has the consonants YHWH (thought originally to have been pronounced Yahweh); the Massoretes, considering the name too sacred to pronounce, placed upon those consonants the points appropriate to one of two other words – *adonai*, my Lord, or *elohim*, God – and the reader was instructed to pronounce not the divine name at all but one of these titles instead. Hence, in the N.E.B., as in the ancient translations, the divine name is rendered LORD and not Yahweh; that the Septuagint also renders YHWH as *Lord* is an indication that this reverential tradition extends back at least to the third century B.C. (For

Jehovah, see p. 160 below.) As an example of a Massoretic correction (or, perhaps, of the simultaneous preservation of two traditions), we may cite Ps. 100: 3,
where the consonantal text reads: 'He has made us, and
not we ourselves'; the Massoretic pointing, however,
instructs the reader to read out: 'He has made us, and we
are his.' The pointing superimposed upon the consonantal text enabled the Massoretes to achieve what they
wished without altering the consonantal text, for that was
regarded by them as sacred and, therefore, unalterable.
The result of superimposed pointing is that the language
that is actually read in the Massoretic Text is not ancient
Hebrew, but Massoretic Hebrew, Hebrew as it was read
by the Rabbis in Massoretic times; yet although what is
read aloud is Massoretic Hebrew, the consonants themselves preserve a much older form of the language. If,
then, the Massoretic Text affords us an accurate indication of how the text was read and understood by the
Massoretes in the ninth and tenth centuries A.D., is there
any way in which we can check the accuracy of the text
which they agreed to preserve? Is there any evidence by
means of which we can trace back further into the past
the text of the Hebrew bible?

Non-Massoretic forms of the Hebrew text

Light is shed upon the pre-Massoretic text of the Hebrew
bible both by earlier surviving manuscripts and by later
manuscripts whose tradition can be shown to be independent of the orthodox (Massoretic) tradition.

The so-called Dead Sea Scrolls (see pp. 101–3), discovered in the caves of Qumran near Jericho from 1947,
are dated generally about 150 B.C.–A.D. 75. They include
one complete scroll of Isaiah and portions or fragments of

every other Old Testament book except Esther. Being eleven centuries older than the earliest manuscripts of the Massoretic Text, their evidence is very significant. By far the most important conclusion reached by scholars from the study of these manuscripts is that they confirm beyond all doubt the general accuracy of the Massoretic Text. Furthermore, although they are unpointed, the way some of the Hebrew consonants have been used in them indicates the beginning of the process of fixing the reading of the text, the process which was eventually to culminate in Massoretic pointing. For example, the word for 'peace' was probably originally written *shlm*; in the Scrolls it was written as *shlwm*, where the *w* indicates an o-sound; and, finally, in the Massoretic Text as *sh^{a}l^{o}m* or *sh^{a}l^{o}wm*.

Important as indicating stages between the Dead Sea Scrolls and the Massoretic Text are the manuscripts and fragments which come from the Geniza of the Old Synagogue in Cairo. (Among these is the Zadokite Fragment, or Damascus Document, see p. 83.) Jewish tradition required that worn-out manuscripts, together with those which differed from the standard text, should be stored in a Geniza (a lumber room) until such time as sufficient number accumulated, when they were ceremonially buried. By good fortune the contents of the Cairo Geniza escaped such burial and have come down to us. Much of this material is in the Cambridge University Library.

A third important witness to the pre-Massoretic text is the Samaritan Pentateuch (see pp. 111–12). The beginning of estrangement between the Samaritans and the main stream of Judaism may be traced back as far as the fourth century B.C.; like the Sadducees, the Samaritans of New

Testament times regarded the Pentateuch alone as canonical, and believed that it indicated Mount Gerizim as God's chosen place of worship (see John 4: 20). This bible of the Samaritan community which has survived into modern times at its ancient location near Nablus represents therefore a textual tradition which stretches back continuously into the early centuries B.C. and is quite independent of orthodox Judaism and Massoretic influence. The text itself is preserved in manuscripts the earliest of which is from the eleventh century A.D. The script of the Samaritan Pentateuch is important because it is a survival of the Old Hebrew script and an indication that this was still used in the early centuries B.C. Again the study of this form of the Hebrew text confirms the general accuracy of the Massoretic Text.

Important information is also provided about the Hebrew text by the ancient 'versions' made from it. As these are translations and do not preserve the actual Hebrew text, very considerable and specialized knowledge is often required in order to make use of them as evidence. They have to be translated back into Hebrew by conjecture from the language concerned, and so such findings must always be more or less tentative. The primary importance of the versions, however, is that they provide early evidence as to what people thought was the meaning of the Hebrew text.

The ancient 'versions' of the Hebrew bible

The ancient translations (usually called *versions*) of the Hebrew bible were made either by communities of Jews who were no longer familiar with Hebrew, or by Christians whose culture and languages were quite distinct from Judaism and Hebrew (although even then some

Hebrew words survived from the Hebrew tradition such as *Amen* and *Hallelujah*). There are four main versions:

The Septuagint, the Vulgate, the Targums and the Peshitta.

(a) *The Septuagint* (frequently abbreviated to LXX) *and other Greek versions*

Jeremiah's reluctant journey to Egypt in the sixth century B.C. (Jer. 43: 7) marks the beginning of the appearance of substantial colonies of Jews in that country. From the fifth century B.C. we have evidence of Jewish soldiers serving as mercenaries in the Persian administration of Egypt. At his death in 323 B.C., the eastern part of Alexander the Great's empire split into two: the Seleucids ruled the northern part from Antioch in Syria, and the Ptolemies in the south ruled Egypt. Greek replaced Aramaic as the official language of diplomacy and commerce, and by the third century B.C. the large number of Jews living in Alexandria were Greek-speaking. A substantial quantity of their commercial and legal correspondence written on papyrus in Greek has survived to the present day by reason of the hot, dry climate of Egypt.

That the need for a translation of the Hebrew scriptures would arise in the synagogues of such Greek-speaking Jews is not surprising, and the Septuagint is an indication of the sort of translations they produced. According to the idealized and legendary account of its origin given in the Letter of Aristeas (about 130 B.C., see also p. 86), king Ptolemy II Philadelphus of Egypt requested the Jerusalem High Priest to authorize a translation of the Law (Pentateuch) for his library. Seventy-two (Latin *Septuaginta* = 'seventy', hence the name, and the abbreviation to LXX) Jewish scholars were sent from Jerusalem to effect the work, and in seventy-two days they emerged with a unified translation. This tall story is held by modern critics to have been devised for propaganda purposes. The writer of the Letter (written some 130 years after Ptolemy II's reign) is likely to have had, among other motives, the desire to re-assert the authority of the Septuagint at a time when it was being subjected to criticism as being not an accurate translation. However, the Letter does corroborate what may be deduced from other evidence, namely that the process of translating the Hebrew bible into Greek started in the third century B.C. The preface to the book of Ecclesiasticus (written in Greek during the latter half of the second century B.C. – see p. 116) indicates that the Law, the Prophets and the 'rest of the writings' had been translated; this may be regarded as a date-before-which the work was complete.

The promulgation and spread of Christianity in Greek in the first century A.D. gave the Septuagint added importance. Indeed many of the New Testament quotations of the Old Testament are Septuagint quotations, one of the more famous being that of Isa. 7: 14, 'The virgin will conceive and bear a son', where the Massoretic Text has 'young woman'. The appropriation and use of the Septuagint by the Church led the Greek-speaking Jews to become increasingly dissatisfied with it and to require improved translations of the Hebrew (from their point of view).

Three such revised translations are known to us.

(1) Aquila, a Jew of Pontus, produced an extremely literal Greek translation of the Massoretic Text in about A.D. 130. So literal was this translation that he abuses the Greek language to reproduce verbal similarities peculiar

to the Hebrew language; and for purposes of religious argument he carefully avoids the translation of the Hebrew word 'Messiah' (= anointed) by the Greek word 'Christ(os)'.

(2) The version of Symmachus is probably from the early third century A.D. Possibly a pupil of the Jewish scholar Rabbi Meir, Symmachus sought to repeat what Aquila had done, but at the same time to write polished, idiomatic Greek. Contemporary Jewish influence may be detected in his softening of some of the more graphic anthropomorphisms (descriptions of God in human terms) of the Old Testament.

(3) Dated late in the second century A.D. (and by some earlier) is Theodotion's thorough revision of the Septuagint with reference to the Hebrew bible. The resulting version constitutes a Greek text far closer to the Massoretic Text than to the Hebrew text which underlies the Septuagint. There is some evidence to suggest that Theodotion was a Christian, and, if this evidence is correct, his version would indicate a desire on the part of Christians, too, for an improved Greek version.

Recent discoveries in Palestine of Greek manuscript fragments of the first century A.D. indicate clearly that attempts at revision of the Septuagint were common at this time. The more literal revisions, of which these manuscripts are evidence, may also be related to the known practice of reproducing the Hebrew text in Greek letters so that those Jews who could not read the Hebrew script might yet 'read' the sacred language. (Some Rabbis required that Jews should be able to recite, for example, Deut. 6: 4 in Hebrew.)

The history of the text of the Septuagint is complicated, and it is not possible here to give an account of it. It may be said, however, that the earliest manuscripts are of the third and fourth centuries A.D., and that a papyrus fragment of the second century B.C. has survived and is in the John Rylands Library in Manchester. Mention must also be made of two important revisions (called 'recensions' by scholars) of the Septuagint text. The first was made by Origen (A.D. 185–254) who, though he continued to regard the Septuagint as the official Old Testament of the Church, was the first Christian scholar to make use of the Hebrew text. Perturbed by the large number of variant (Septuagint) manuscripts, he produced his *Hexapla* with six columns to the page, containing:

(1) the Hebrew text in Hebrew letters; (2) the Hebrew text written in Greek letters; (3) Aquila; (4) Symmachus; (5) the Septuagint; (6) Theodotion.

The *Hexapla* has survived only in fragments and quotations, though the fifth column became widely popular and was regarded as an authoritative text of the Septuagint. Secondly, in about A.D. 310, and independently of Origen, Lucian of Antioch sought to revise the text of the Septuagint known to him in the interests of 'clarity and completeness'. His revision has certain similarities to that quoted by Josephus (A.D. 37–100), and is important as an early witness to the text of the Septuagint, or just possibly to the text of a Greek version which is independent of the Septuagint.

The Septuagint is the most important of the versions for at least four reasons:

(1) It is the oldest.

(2) It witnesses to a Hebrew text which was current in Egypt in the early centuries B.C., and which is in some respects different from the Massoretic Text (for example,

the chapters of the book of Jeremiah are in a quite different order).

(3) It is an early translation into a non-Semitic language. It therefore provides scholars with early evidence as to what, for example, Greek-speaking Jews thought was the meaning of the Hebrew.

(4) It was *the* Old Testament of the early Church.

Finally it should be noted that the books of the Apocrypha (see chapter 4) have come down to us in the Septuagint text and are not present in the Massoretic Text. It had long been known that the original language of some of these books was Hebrew; the preface to Ecclesiasticus explicitly says that that book is a translation, and in the nineteenth century and more recently at Masada by the Dead Sea, Hebrew manuscripts of Ecclesiasticus have actually been discovered. That the Apocryphal books do not appear in the Massoretic Text is one of the indications that they were not regarded as canonical by orthodox Judaism.

(b) *The Vulgate*

As Christianity spread westwards through the Roman empire in the early centuries A.D. the need arose for a Latin version of the bible. This was more immediately felt in North Africa where Latin was the official language and to which Latin-speaking missionaries went from Italy in the early second century. In Rome, by contrast, until at least A.D. 150 the language of Christians remained predominantly Greek.

The first Latin translations made in North Africa were from the Septuagint, still regarded as the bible of the Church. They are known to us only from manuscript fragments and from quotations in the works of North

African Christian writers of the time. Such translations are usually named the *Old Latin* versions, and their importance is as a witness to the current Septuagint text rather than to the Hebrew.

In 382 Pope Damasus requested the scholar Jerome to revise the current Latin bible. For the first five years Jerome devoted his attention to the New Testament and to the Psalms. Doing precisely what his patron requested, he revised and polished the current (Old) Latin text. The Psalter, the first that he produced, is named the Roman Psalter and to this day it is used in St Peter's, Rome and in St Mark's, Venice. (Some scholars urge that this psalter is an Old Latin psalter wrongly attributed to Jerome.)

In about 390 Jerome went to Bethlehem and, passing through Caesarea, had the opportunity of consulting Origen's *Hexapla*. From the fifth column (the Septuagint) he made a second revision of the Psalter, called the Gallican Psalter because it was early adopted by the churches of Gaul. The Gallican Psalter was subsequently very highly regarded by the whole Western Church and became the official version of the Psalms. For this reason it is the text preserved in printed editions of the Vulgate, and the text from which Coverdale made his English version in 1535. To this day it is Coverdale's version of the Gallican Psalter that is printed in the Book of Common Prayer.

In Bethlehem Jerome, coming to the conclusion that the Hebrew was the true Old Testament text, made himself familiar with the Hebrew language and Rabbinic methods. By 405 he had completed a new Latin translation of the Hebrew text in forceful, idiomatic language and based on the principle that general sense was more important than the literal translation of single words. It is this version that was subsequently called the Vulgate (Latin *vulgata editio* = 'standard/official version'). The new version naturally included a translation of the Psalms, the third to be associated with the name of Jerome. But this one, called the Psalter according to the Hebrews, never displaced the Gallican Psalter by reason of the high esteem enjoyed by the latter. Opposition to Jerome for presuming to undermine the position of the Septuagint was at first considerable, yet by the end of his life (420) it had largely died down. Subsequently the Vulgate became the official bible of the Western (Roman Catholic) Church (but see above as to the Psalms).

Jerome, influenced by Jewish (Rabbinic) views, was not at first inclined to translate the books of the Apocrypha which were not, in any case, apparently then known in Hebrew. Under the pressure of the Roman clergy, however, and on the argument that the Septuagint was still *the* bible of the Church, he agreed to compromise by translating Aramaic versions of Tobit and Judith, and by retaining the rest of the Apocrypha in an Old Latin version.

The Vulgate is of importance for five main reasons:

(1) It marks the first recognition by the Church of the primacy of the Hebrew text.

(2) It is a witness to the Hebrew text as it was at the end of the fourth century A.D. (500 years before the Massoretic Text).

(3) It is the best (the most coherent) of the ancient versions.

(4) The fact that Jerome was taught Hebrew by contemporary Rabbis allows us to infer that the Vulgate may preserve early Jewish traditions, concerning the meaning of Hebrew words.

(5) It had a great influence upon Western Christendom during the Middle Ages and thereafter.

(c) *The Targums*

It is strictly speaking wrong to speak of one *Targum*, for a number of *Targums* are known to us. The gradual replacement of Hebrew by Aramaic as the popular language of Palestinian Jews from the sixth century B.C. onwards has been described above (pp. 139–42). Just as the need had arisen for a Greek translation of the Law among Egyptian Jews of the early centuries B.C., so in Palestine from about the fourth century B.C. Aramaic translations of the Hebrew bible were required so that the Jews might learn their faith and history. Jewish tradition relates that the writing of such translations was at first forbidden, and that only oral translation by a synagogue translator was allowed; further this was to be done verse by verse in the case of the Law and every three verses in the case of the Prophets. It is these translations that are known as Targums (Hebrew *Targum* = 'translation').

By contrast to the early Christian view that the Septuagint was *the* (inspired) bible, Jewish tradition always remained firmly convinced that the Hebrew alone constituted scripture. The idea of literal translation was consequently in some ways repugnant to Jews; for it involved a sort of contamination of the real (Hebrew) bible. On the other hand, the explanation and interpretation of scripture (and more especially of the Law) was always held in the highest esteem by Judaism. If then literal translation was dangerous, it remained possible to give an Aramaic explanation of previously read Hebrew verses; such a solution upheld the principle that the Hebrew constituted *the* bible. The Talmud (the official repository of Jewish tradition) gives the following excellent example of what a proper Targum should be: to translate literally Exod. 24: 10 'and they saw the God of Israel' would be to mislead people because no one has ever seen God; the correct Targum (translation *and* explanation) is 'and they saw the glory of the God of Israel' (*B. Kiddushin* 49 *a*). According to similar principles the anthropomorphisms of the Hebrew bible are consistently avoided in proper Targum; for example, Adam and Eve do not 'hear the Lord God walking in the garden at the time of the evening breeze', they hear 'the voice of the Word of the Lord God...'. Furthermore, because explanation is consciously interwoven with translation, the situations and problems of the translator and his audience are 'read back' into the biblical past; thus, the quite general repentance urged by Isa. 2: 5 becomes in the Targum the particular repentance of returning to the observance of the (Pharisaic) Law.

Because the Targums are at once translation, explanation and sermon, they have to be used with extreme caution as a witness to the Hebrew text. On the other hand they are evidence as to the way in which Palestinian and Babylonian Jews understood the Hebrew bible in the early centuries A.D. Further, as the Targums we possess are based upon earlier oral tradition, they indicate the way in which scripture was interpreted by Palestinian Jews at the time of Christ, and are therefore of great importance to New Testament scholars.

Targums to all books of the Old Testament (except Daniel and Ezra, which are already written partly in Aramaic) are known to us. The earliest surviving example of a Targum is a fragment of Job found amongst the Dead Sea Scrolls. 'Eli, Eli, lema sabachthani?', the quotation of

Ps. 22: 1 in Matt. 27: 46 and Mark 15: 34, is also thought to have been derived from a contemporary Palestinian Targum.

The authoritative Targums are the Targum of Onkelos (containing the Law) and the Targum of Jonathan (containing the Prophets), dated in the fifth century A.D., and regarded as official by Judaism from that time. The material, though certainly old and Palestinian in origin, was transmitted and edited by Babylonian Jews (forerunners of the Massoretes) and their stamp has clearly been left upon it. The names Onkelos and Jonathan are thought to be Aramaic forms of Aquila and Theodotion, with whom the Targums were erroneously associated.

Of considerable interest are manuscripts found in the Cairo Geniza (called collectively the Palestinian Targum) and a manuscript recently discovered in the Vatican Library, called Neofiti I. Their importance derives from the fact that they are free from Babylonian editorial activity and, therefore, witness more accurately to the form of Aramaic written in Palestine, and consequently to genuine Palestinian Targums.

(d) *The Peshitta*

The various dialects of the Aramaic language are divided into two main groups: Western Aramaic (usually called simply 'Aramaic') and Eastern Aramaic. Syriac is one of the most important dialects of Eastern Aramaic; it has its own script (in three separate forms) and it is still spoken by small groups of Syrian Christians in the Near East.

By the end of the first century A.D. Syriac was spoken in the Euphrates valley and over a wide area of western Asia. More particularly it was the language of the Christian church at Edessa, which flourished between the

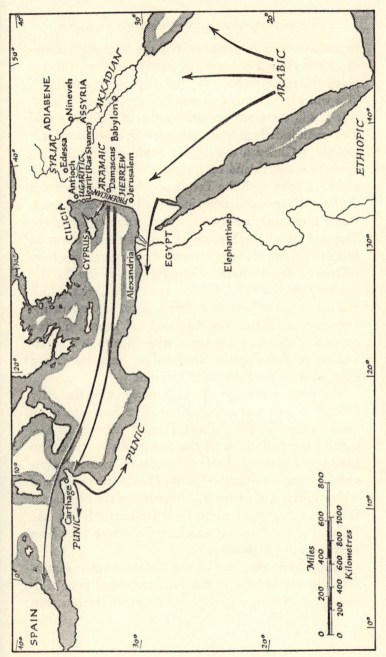

6. The spread of the Semitic languages

second and seventh centuries. It is the bible (Old Testament and New Testament) of this Syrian church that is given the name Peshitta (Syriac = 'plain' [translation]. The word is sometimes written Peshitto).

It is still far from certain whether the Peshitta Old Testament is derived from earlier Jewish translations or is entirely a Christian translation. Some parts of it (particularly Proverbs and Ezekiel) display to a large extent verbal identity with the Targums, while others (such as the Psalms) are considerably influenced by the Septuagint. But it is certainly not overall a translation either of the Targums or of the Septuagint, but of the Hebrew. In order to explain the way in which the Targums may have influenced the Peshitta, scholars point to the Syriac-speaking province of Adiabene, east of the Tigris, which was converted to Judaism before A.D. 70. In view of the known contacts between Adiabene and Jerusalem it is a reasonable inference that those who undertook a Syriac version of the scriptures in Adiabene may have been influenced by the Palestinian Targums.

The general prestige of the Septuagint in the early Church is sufficient explanation of its influence upon some passages of the Peshitta. Further attempts to harmonize the Peshitta with the Septuagint are likely to have taken place in the fourth century, when Christianity became the official religion of the Roman empire of which Edessa was a part. The influence of the Septuagint is more apparent in those Old Testament books like Psalms and the Prophets which are known to have been important to Christianity.

This uneven character of the Peshitta renders impossible a simple description of it. Furthermore, although it is an important witness to the pre-Massoretic Hebrew text, precise evaluation of each relevant part is a necessary prelude to its being used in this way. As a translation of the Old Testament into another Semitic language, and as the bible of the ancient Syrian Church, the version has very considerable interest.

English versions of the Bible

It remains to describe briefly the history of the Bible (and especially the Old Testament) in English: when that too is in the reader's mind he will be in a position fully to appreciate the principles adopted by the translators of the New English Bible.

The beginnings of the Bible in English may be traced back to the 'Venerable' Bede (673–735) who is said to have translated the Fourth Gospel in the latter part of his life. Of the books of the Old Testament the first to be translated into English was the Psalter; interlinear translations of the Gallican Psalter (that transmitted by the Vulgate) are known from the ninth and tenth centuries.

King Alfred's Laws contain a translation of Exod. 20–23, and his name is also associated with a prose translation of Psalms 1–50. Translations of various other Old Testament passages are contained in the homilies of Aelfric, abbot of Eynsham in the tenth century.

The first more-or-less complete translation of the Vulgate Old Testament into English dates from the fourteenth century and is associated with the name of Wycliffe, though the work was in fact done by Nicholas of Hereford and John Purvey. The Council of Oxford (1407) condemned this version and forbade the making of any new translations, a decision which may be held to reflect the desire of the pre-Reformation Church to maintain the primacy of the Vulgate.

The invention of printing gave great impetus to the study and translation of the Bible. The Vulgate was first printed in 1456, and the Massoretic Text in 1488. In 1525 William Tyndale, one of the early reformers, published his English New Testament, and in 1529 translated the Pentateuch and other passages of the Old Testament from the Hebrew. His work is an original translation, though he was influenced both by the Vulgate and by Luther's German version (finally published in 1534). We may note that Tyndale preferred to render the divine name exactly as it appears in the Massoretic Text; he reproduced the grammatically impossible combination of the consonants YHWH with the vowels of ᵃDᵒNᵃY (my Lord), giving YᵃHᵒWᵃH. The word, modified to Jehovah, has been used subsequently in most English versions (the N.E.B. included) at Exod. 3: 15, 6: 3 and to render some place-names (for example Jehovah-jireh in Gen. 22: 14).

Miles Coverdale translated the whole Bible in 1535 and dedicated the work to Henry VIII. Knowing no Hebrew, Coverdale utilized the work of Tyndale and translated the other books of the Old Testament from the Vulgate and from the German versions of Luther and Zwingli. His version of the Psalms is particularly well known, and has remained in use as the Psalter of the Book of Common Prayer. (A fine revision of Coverdale's Psalter upon the basis of modern scholarship was published in 1963 under the title *The Revised Psalter*.) The Great Bible of 1539 is a revision of Coverdale's Bible.

The Protestant exiles of Mary's reign published in Geneva another English translation of the Bible in 1560, and this version, known as the Geneva Bible, achieved great popularity during the reign of Elizabeth I. Lacking, however, royal authorization and ecclesiastical favour, the Geneva Bible was supplanted by a revision of the Great Bible, known as the Bishops' Bible, which, although having the Great Bible as its basis, was considerably influenced by reference to the original languages.

As a result of the Hampton Court Conference of 1604, James I commissioned the undertaking of a new version of the complete Bible. The result was the publication in 1611 of the Authorized Version (A.V.), which by reason of its magnificent language has remained ever since the most loved and used English Bible. The fifty-four theologians who did the work used the Bishops' Bible as the basis for their revision, but took into account both earlier English versions and the best Hebrew and Greek editions then available. Within fifty years the version displaced all earlier ones and in 1662 the text of the A.V. was the one which was used for the Epistles and Gospels of the Book of Common Prayer. The A.V. achieved recognition not only in England, but spread through all the English colonies including North America, where to this day it is known as the King James Version.

The main subsequent revisions are the Revised Version (R.V.) published in England in 1885, and the Revised Standard Version (R.S.V.) published in the U.S.A. in 1952. Both works arose as a result of the rapid growth of biblical scholarship in the nineteenth and twentieth centuries, and the resulting realization of mistakes and inconsistencies in the A.V. The R.V., which was a conservative revision, never achieved wide popularity, though its accuracy and marginal notes made it very useful to those studying the original languages. The R.S.V., based ultimately on the R.V., represents another stage in the process of improving translations in the light of continued biblical research. By avoiding both archaic English and also words that had not been in use for more than 100 years, the R.S.V. marks the beginning of the desire to modify the traditional English of the Authorized Version. (For Roman Catholic translations, see pp. 129–30.)

In 1946 the major British denominations (with the exception of the Roman Catholic Church) agreed at the suggestion of the Church of Scotland to make a completely new and official translation of the Bible 'in the language of the present day', and upon the basis of the most up-to-date scholarship. Three panels were appointed to translate from the original languages the Old Testament, the Apocrypha and the New Testament respectively. The New Testament was published in 1961, and the Old Testament and Apocrypha in 1970; the version was named the New English Bible (N.E.B.).

The principles and problems of translating
the Old Testament

The importance of the N.E.B. as a translation of the Old Testament lies in the fact that it is based upon the most up-to-date scholarship and that it is a *new* translation. This independence has made possible the maximum utilization of the results of modern research. The last century or so has seen a very considerable increase in our knowledge of the languages, customs and institutions of the ancient Near East, as well as of the history of the Old Testament text. The twentieth-century translators of the Old Testament are therefore able to make use of knowledge which was simply not available to their predecessors – the kind of knowledge which this chapter has attempted to describe.

It has been estimated that the Massoretic Text makes use of some 8,000 Hebrew words; of these some 2,000 occur only once. By contrast the works of Shakespeare

are said to utilize 21,000, all of which occur elsewhere. In English there is a large literature contemporary with and preceding Shakespeare; with the exception of the Old Testament and a few inscriptions, no other work in Hebrew has survived from biblical times. Shakespeare's works, together with those of contemporary and preceding English writers, refer to many subjects; the literature of the Old Testament is limited in its subject-matter, and there is little with which to compare it. The reader will appreciate that these facts make the problem of translating the Old Testament very considerable. Furthermore, not only are there problems associated with the meaning and reference of words, there are also problems raised by textual corruption: it is not surprising that texts copied and recopied over some 2,000 years should contain errors. So it is sometimes impossible for the translator to determine whether the text of a verse of the Massoretic Text contains an error, or whether it contains words or phrases whose meaning is now lost to him.

In seeking to solve such problems the modern translator has been considerably helped by comparing various Semitic languages and by continued study of the text and versions of the Old Testament. The very close relationship of Semitic languages has been described above. While, therefore, it is true that much is still unknown to us of the vocabulary of ancient Hebrew, we are constantly learning more about it from a study of other Semitic languages. For example, the translators of the A.V., R.V., and R.S.V. thought that there was one Hebrew word *yd'* meaning 'to know'; accordingly they translated the phrase in Judg. 16: 9 which speaks of an unsuccessful attempt by Delilah to betray Samson: 'So his strength was not known.' With the help of Arabic, however, it has become clear that there were two separate words in ancient Hebrew, spelt in the same way, one meaning 'to know', the other meaning 'to be tamed', 'to be quiet'. (In English, too, there are words spelt in the same way which have separate meanings: for example, a dog's *lead* and *lead* = a metal.) Therefore the N.E.B. rightly translates Judg. 16: 9 'And his strength was not tamed'. The Peshitta in fact translates the phrase in a way very similar to the N.E.B., and we may conclude that the Peshitta translators also knew that two separate words lay behind the one spelling *yd'*.

When the Massoretic Text appears to contain an error the translator tries to find firm evidence that there is one in fact, and to establish what the text was before the error crept in. An example of textual corruption is in the Massoretic Text of Isa. 41: 27, where the Hebrew words as they stand are quite unintelligible, but one of the Dead Sea Scrolls indicates that a letter has at some stage dropped out of the Massoretic Text (perhaps by a scribe's mistake). When the reading of the Scroll is adopted, and the text thereby restored, the meaning of the words becomes quite clear: 'Here is one who will speak first as advocate for Zion' (so the N.E.B.; the A.V. reads, 'The first shall say to Zion, "Behold, behold them"').

Archaeological discovery has also helped the modern Old Testament translator. Finds from Syria, Babylon, Assyria and Egypt have all contributed to our understanding of the life and customs of ancient Israel, and consequently to the improvement of Old Testament translation. For example, the phrase in Ezek. 8: 17, translated in the N.E.B. 'while they seek to appease me', means literally 'while they hold twigs to their nostrils'. A sculpture from Assyria depicts sun worshippers holding sticks to their faces as a sign of supplication. The curious phrase of Ezekiel can therefore be confirmed as accurate, and in translation the meaning can be made clear.

But if modern knowledge substantially helps the twentieth-century translator, it also raises new problems for him. The apparent simplicity of many Hebrew words and expressions is now seen to disguise alternative meanings hitherto unknown. Thus, in Psalm 23 there is the famous phrase, 'the valley of the shadow of death'. It is now appreciated more fully that the word *death* was used in idiomatic Hebrew as an intensive, just as it is in English in the phrase 'a deadly pain'. It is then very likely that the phrase in Psalm 23 means the *valley of the darkest shadow*, and there is no reference to death at all. Again, there is now evidence that the word *god* was used in the same way as an intensive. In Gen. 1:2 the translator is faced with the word *god* and a word which can mean either *wind* or *spirit*. Is he then to translate 'the Spirit of God hovered over the surface of the waters' or 'a mighty wind that swept over the surface of the waters'? The translators of the N.E.B. chose the latter alternative. They may well be right. But in making that choice and others like it they may be said to have given us not merely a New English Bible, but a new *bible*, which differs very considerably from previous and familiar bibles.

So we return to our starting-point: Is the N.E.B. now THE BIBLE? What this chapter has attempted to show is that the N.E.B. is one more, and, to date, the most accurate and scholarly, strand in the continuing tradition.

6

THE OLD TESTAMENT FOR JEWS AND CHRISTIANS TODAY

Behind the Old Testament as we know it lie centuries of tradition, transmission, translation and criticism. Today it is read in churches, set for examination texts and made the subject of sermons. It also turns out to be the source of expressions like 'the apple of one's eye', 'feet of clay', 'bricks without straw', and 'fly in the ointment'. But has it any real value, or relevance, or even interest other than that of the purely academic variety, for the twentieth century?

It may help us to answer this question if we look at its place and significance within two of the great religious communities which share it as a heritage: Judaism and Christianity. (Its position within Islamic tradition, while important, is more subordinate.)

THE PLACE OF THE SCRIPTURES IN JUDAISM

Scriptural interpretation

By tradition, study of and speculation about the scriptures goes back to the time of Ezra or even earlier. Deut. 6: 6–8 says:

These commandments which I give you this day are to be kept in your heart; you shall repeat them to your sons, and speak of them indoors and out of doors, when you lie down and when you rise. Bind them as a sign on the hand and wear them as a phylactery on the forehead; write them up on the door-posts of your houses and on your gates.

The 'you' here is singular; this can be interpreted as a call to private and individual study. According to Neh. 8:7,8:

(They) expounded the law to the people while they remained in their places. They read from the book of the law of God clearly, made its sense plain and gave instruction in what was read.

In Jewish tradition 'they' – that is, Ezra and his assistants – stood in the line of interpreters who down the centuries into the Christian era studied the Law, explained it and related it to new situations.

This kind of interpretation was fostered by the Pharisees (the Sadducees, by contrast, took a more rigid and literal line – and, perhaps significantly, did not survive beyond the end of the first century A.D.), and is known as the Rabbinical tradition (*Rabbi* = literally 'my master'). The underlying principle was that the scriptures were of priceless worth and high inspiration. The Torah was the core; every word and syllable had equal authority, there were no contradictions or discrepancies, nor, since it had been given to Moses, was there any question of gradual or progressive revelation. The Prophets and the Writings explained it, and often texts were used in threes, one from the Torah, then one from the Prophets and one from the Writings in support. One result of this approach was that verses tended to be taken out of their historical contexts and linked with other verses likewise detached. Passages so used are called 'proof texts'; as we shall see, some of the New Testament writers made use of this method of interpretation.

Over the years Rabbis tended to specialize in one or other of two main aspects of Jewish tradition. There were those whose chief concern was with observances – that is, religious or civil law. The technical term for these matters is *Halakah* (from the Hebrew *halak*, 'to go', 'to walk'), which came to be used in the sense first of 'way' and 'guidance', then of 'habit' or 'practice'. The Halakah, then, consists of laws or legal decisions, sometimes based directly on scripture, sometimes cited independently though often with the claim that they can if necessary be justified from the Bible. (It must be remembered that 'Bible' here means what Christians call the Old Testament but Jews call the *Tanak* – see p. 108.) In a wider sense 'Halakah' can describe the whole of Jewish legal tradition – usages, customs, decrees and opinions. Its development was the result of the need to think out how the principles and commandments of the Torah should be applied in changing circumstances over the centuries.

Other teachers were particularly interested in the nonlegal aspects of Judaism, for which the word is *Haggadah*, from *haggid*, 'to report', or 'to explain'. This could include narrative, homily, astrology, medicine, magic and mysticism. Like Halakah, Haggadah may or may not be based directly on biblical material, but it differs in that it is a popular rather than a technical type of exegesis. Halakah and Haggadah have been described as 'law' and 'lore'.

General exposition and explanation, particularly of scripture, is called *Midrash* (from *darash*, 'to study', or 'to investigate'). Unlike *peshat*, which is simple and literal interpretation, it goes deeply into the text, studies it from all sides, and derives explanations which are not immediately apparent. It can be linked with both Halakah and Haggadah. *Midrashic Halakah* may take an accepted Halakah and verify it from the scriptures, or it may begin the other way round by interpreting and sometimes elaborating laws which are already in the Bible, and deciding under what circumstances they are to be applied and what are likely to be the consequences. Num. 9: 10 decrees that if at Passover time a man is 'ritually unclean through contact with a corpse, or if he is away on a long journey', he shall celebrate the feast a month later. An early Midrashic Halakah on the verse declares that anyone who is unclean *for any reason whatsoever* must postpone his celebration. This is the result of a very slight alteration to the text, which allows 'away on a long journey' to be interpreted as 'afar off' – that is, far from the temple, in the sense of being ritually unclean. During the first and second centuries of the Christian era, Midrashic Halakah became even more specific in its interpretations; one of these later comments on the same verse in Numbers retains 'away on a long journey', but specifies exactly how far away a man must be before he is excluded from the Passover.

Midrashic Haggadah applies much the same treatment to the non-legal parts of the Old Testament; it is moral and edifying in tone, and lacking the legal framework of Midrashic Halakah is freer and more imaginative. This kind of exegesis is cited in 1 Cor. 10: 4 when Paul, describing the wilderness wanderings of the children of Israel after the exodus, mentions 'the supernatural rock that accompanied their travels' – referring to the Rabbinic idea that the two accounts of water being brought from a rock by Moses (Exod. 17: 6, Num. 20: 2–13) could be explained by the rock having moved with the Israelites from one place to another. Or on Gen. 1: 26 *Bereshit Rabbah*, one of the oldest commentaries, taught: 'And God said, "Let us make man"'... with whom did he take counsel? Rabbi Joshua ben Levi said "He consulted the works of the heaven and the earth, like a king who has two counsellors". Rabbi Samuel ben Nathan said "He took counsel with the work of every day of creation".'

All this tradition, Halakah, Haggadah and Midrash, was for centuries transmitted mainly by word of mouth and associated with individual Rabbis such as Simeon ben Shetach, Hillel and Shammai in the first century B.C. and Akiba in the second century A.D.; at what stage was the enormous task of recording and codifying it attempted? There are two key words here, *Mishnah* and *Talmud*.

The Mishnah (see pp. 96-7) arose from the need to systematize the mass of legal tradition, both biblical and non-biblical. The name itself comes from *shanah*, originally 'to repeat' and in post-biblical Hebrew 'to teach' or 'to learn'. Attempts to reduce to some sort of order the Law and the oral tradition surrounding it may have begun in the time of Hillel and Shammai, with the object of providing teachers with a textbook for their classes and a handbook for themselves. Then for a time, after the fall of Jerusalem in A.D. 70, careful doctrinal study lapsed somewhat; Halakoth (Hebrew plural of Halakah) were disputed or forgotten. After the discussions associated with Jamnia (see pp. 106-7), further efforts were made to encourage uniformity of doctrine. Various collections were begun, including one by Rabbi Akiba, but the real definitive work was undertaken by Rabbi Judah (the codifier *par excellence*, known as 'the Prince'), and according to tradition completed in written form only in his extreme old age at the end of the second century A.D.

The Mishnah recorded for posterity that 'fence about the Law' erected by teachers traditionally going back to Ezra, who were without exception concerned that its essential features should be protected, explained and applied to all parts of life. It forms the core of an even larger work, the *Talmud*, from *limmēd*, 'to teach', therefore meaning literally 'teaching'. The name Talmud can be applied loosely to any kind of instruction or exegesis from the text of the Bible, or to all three branches of traditional interpretation together – Halakah, Haggadah and Midrash. But more specifically it is the name for two works, or, perhaps more accurately, one work with two branches, the Palestinian Talmud and the Babylonian Talmud. Each has the Mishnah as its basis; its other part is called *Gemara* (lit. 'memorizing', from *gamar*, 'to polish', 'to complete'), that is, commentary on the Mishnah. The Palestinian Gemara is the record of the discussions of scholars in Palestine, and was completed about A.D. 400; the Babylonian Gemara is a similar record of the work of Babylonian scholars, and was completed about A.D. 500. Of the two the latter is the more widely read and studied. The two versions are always printed separately; their composition can be set out in equation form:

The Mishnah + the Palestinian Gemara
$$= \text{the Palestinian Talmud}$$
The Mishnah + the Babylonian Gemara
$$= \text{the Babylonian Talmud}$$

It is possible to regard this wealth of tradition with amazement and even trepidation; to wonder how anyone can possibly find a way through its complexities and ramifications. Shammai, a near-contemporary of Jesus, must have done nothing to dispel this impression when, asked to give a summary of the Law which a man could hear whilst balancing on one leg, he sent the enquirer about his business. More profitable because more perceptive was the reply of Hillel to the same question. He quoted a negative (and some might say more realistic) version of the Golden Rule, 'What is displeasing to yourself, do not do to others', and added, 'All the rest is commentary – go and learn.'

Here is the root of the matter – the single principle from which all else derives. Yet when we have grasped it we need to apply it. Then 'all the rest' falls into place as the necessary, constant, detailed working-out of this basic principle.

The Rabbinical tradition did not, of course, represent the only Jewish way of studying the scriptures in the early Christian era. The Community at Qumran was concerned to keep the Law according to its own interpretation, but it was also deeply interested in prophecy, which it claimed to see fulfilled in contemporary events. One of the most famous of the Dead Sea Scrolls, the Commentary on Habakkuk, illustrates this emphasis on relevance. For instance, the Chaldaeans of Hab. 1, who were probably the Babylonians, seen by the prophet as the instrument of God's coming judgement on Judah, in the Commentary become the 'Kittim', the hated occupiers of Judaea (whether Greeks or more particularly Romans), in the Community's own day. So the comment on Hab. 1: 7, which describes the Chaldaeans:

> Terror and awe go with them;
> their justice and judgement are of their own making,

is 'This concerns the Kittim, who inspire all the nations with fear . . . All their evil plotting is done with intention, and they deal with all the nations in cunning and guile.'

Different again was the attitude of the large numbers of Greek-speaking Jews outside Palestine, whose Bible was not the Hebrew text but the Septuagint and who, as the Letter of Aristeas shows, tended to regard the translation itself as divinely inspired. One of the most famous of these Hellenistic Jews was Philo of Alexandria (see chapter 4). Philo was a loyal Jew who kept the Law of Moses and had no doubt been influenced by Rabbinic ideas in drawing the conclusion that it could be interpreted in a variety of ways. But at the same time he was deeply indebted to Greek ideas and to the practice of giving to texts the meaning of allegories – that is, of reading a figurative interpretation into every detail. The outcome was an allegorical interpretation of the Old Testament, as in his commentaries on Genesis and the Law of Moses, together with an emphasis on Greek philosophical ideas relating to the meaning of the universe and of life. He believed that Judaism was the true and final religion and that the Law of Moses contained all that Greek philosophy had to teach. Working on the basis of these convictions he did much to bring Greek and Jewish ideas to terms.

But the Qumran Community disappeared, and its literature lay hidden for nearly two thousand years, whilst the Christian predilection for the Septuagint led to its abandonment by the Jews (see p. 148). It is the Rabbinical tradition which not only provided the foundation for Jewish studies in the early Christian era, but has also had the most profound and lasting influence on them during the intervening centuries.

Contemporary Judaism

For Judaism today the Hebrew Bible is the great treasury of religious truth, enshrining the experience of the past and pointing the way to right living in the present and the future. Its language is the language of worship in the Orthodox (traditional) synagogues, and in part that of the Reform and Liberal congregations, who have shortened and simplified forms of service. The heart of the matter is still the Torah, and here there are differences of emphasis when its provisions are applied to modern life. The Orthodox Jew holds a high view of inspiration; not only is the Law the work of Moses, it is the Word of God. Therefore as far as possible it is kept to the letter – the Sabbath, the dietary laws and the family customs are observed. With it in authority go the Mishnah and the pronouncements of Rabbis down to the present day – the latter known as *responsa* because they record answers given to questions put by congregations. A recent *responsum* is the decision of the Ashkenazi Chief Rabbi of Israel to permit the use of certain types of microphone in the synagogue on the Sabbath. *The Jewish Chronicle* of 14 August 1970, commenting on the new thinking behind this ruling, recalls that 'One of our foremost halakic authorities pronounced some years ago that the microphone devices available were not fit for use on the Sabbath, nor would any device invented in the future be suitable'.

Reform Judaism, the movement begun in England in the mid-nineteenth century, is more flexible; it accepts the moral force of the principles underlying the Torah, but tries to adapt it to modern requirements, taking into account the findings of scientific research and biblical criticism. It argues that many specific provisions need no longer be taken literally because the conditions which they were intended to meet have ceased to exist. For example, Exod. 23: 19, 'You shall not boil a kid in its mother's milk', has led to the custom of separating all milk and meat dishes, even to the utensils used in preparing and eating them. (Food prepared in accordance with this and the other dietary laws is called *kosher*, meaning 'right', or 'good'.) The Orthodox Jew would argue that the very observance of this reminds him that eating and drinking are a part of the sanctity of life lived in obedience to the will of God, and are to be done to his glory. The Reform Jew, on the other hand, whilst he would accept the religious principle behind this regulation and would therefore quite probably observe it, would hesitate to insist that it must be kept to the letter at all times and by everyone. A member of a Liberal congregation (Liberal Judaism is the outcome of the re-thinking of biblical and theological questions which arose during the early part of the twentieth century) would be less concerned with the letter of the Law than either the Orthodox or the Reform Jew, whilst Conservative Judaism (an offshoot of Orthodoxy in the United States) would take a more central position, giving weight to scholarly criticism but at the same time, as far as is consistent, trying to preserve the Orthodox way of life.

When it comes to non-legal parts of the Pentateuch, as well as to the Prophets and the Writings, there is throughout Judaism a great deal of freedom in interpretation and a fairly realistic view of the comparative merits of different books and passages. Even in the Rabbinical literature some unevenness in quality is admitted; thus 'Isaiah and Ezekiel both saw the king, but Isaiah like one that dwelleth in a city, Ezekiel like a villager' – in other words, both were inspired, but the difference in their intellectual and spiritual powers was reflected in their message. At the present time scholarly opinion can range from conservative to radical, but there is no officially prescribed or generally accepted attitude.

For the devout Jew, Deut. 6: 4, 'Hear, O Israel, the LORD is our God, one LORD, and you must love the LORD your God with all your heart and soul and strength', known as the *Shema* after its first Hebrew word, is the foundation of his whole life. In his home, the instructions which follow, 'These commandments which I give you this day are to be kept in your heart; you shall repeat them to your sons, and speak of them indoors and out of doors, when you lie down and when you rise', are faithfully obeyed. The children are taught the Shema, and a visual reminder of its centrality is the *Mezuzah* (literally 'doorpost'), a small wooden or metal container fixed to the right-hand side of the door, and containing a slip of parchment on which this and other verses from Deut. 6 (4-9, 11, 13-21) are written. So the command to 'write (these words) up on the door-posts of your houses and on your gates' (Deut. 6: 9) is kept to the letter; all who go in and out are made aware of the vital importance of the Law.

In worship the scriptures have a central place. A reading from the Torah is obligatory; in an Orthodox synagogue it is read by rote throughout the year; when Deuteronomy is finished, Genesis is begun again. In the reading the traditional chanting, or *cantillation*, is used. All types of service have a second reading from the Prophets; the Writings are represented by the Psalms, which, as in the Anglican service, form part of the prayer book. Commentaries are important; many members of an Orthodox congregation will have with them a copy of the great commentary by Rabbi Shlomo Yitzchake (1040–1105) (known as 'Rashi' from his initials); other congregations make use of more modern works, such as that by Rabbi J. H. Hertz.

In addition to the teaching in the home, the children of practising Jewish families are instructed in the scriptures in the synagogue on Sunday mornings. As well as acquiring some knowledge of Hebrew and of the biblical text (learning by heart, in addition to the Shema, is included) they may be introduced to the Mishnah and, according to ability and to the degree of orthodoxy, to more advanced study of the Talmud. The work of these synagogue classes is examined; the syllabus of the London Board of Jewish Religious Education includes for children under fourteen translation from the Hebrew of the Old Testament and Rabbinic works, unseen re-translation from English into Hebrew, knowledge of Jewish faith and practice, the history of ancient Israel and of Judaism, and the geography of the Holy Land and of the modern State of Israel.

So for the practising Jew there is no question of the scriptures being outdated. They are an integral part of his home, the centre of his worship, and an essential element in his education. Indeed the Torah and the principles which it embodies form the whole foundation of his way of life. For him the words of the Psalmist are still true.

The fear of the LORD is pure and abides for ever.
The LORD's decrees are true and righteous every one,
more to be desired than gold, pure gold in plenty,
sweeter than syrup or honey from the comb.
It is these that give thy servant warning,
and he who keeps them wins a great reward (Ps. 19: 9–11)..

THE PLACE OF THE OLD TESTAMENT
IN THE CHRISTIAN COMMUNITY

The Old Testament in the New

The Old Testament was the Bible of the very first Christians, and since they were Jews its authority and inspiration were taken for granted. But a little later, when the New Testament books were coming into being, their authors and editors, had they stopped to put their thoughts into words, might have asked themselves, 'How can the scriptures which we know relate to the life, death and resurrection of Jesus of Nazareth – those tremendous events which we are trying to interpret? And what is the place of these same scriptures in the new way of life which men call Christianity?'

The actual *amount* of Old Testament material which the New Testament writers used gives little indication of any consistent answers. In some parts of the New Testament, such as Acts 7 or the Gospel according to Matthew, it is frequently referred to or quoted; in others, such as the Epistles of John, it is hardly mentioned. On the other hand, the *selection* of references may be significant; although the Pentateuch is well represented, most of the quotations come from the Prophets and the Writings. It is often argued that this points to a greater interest in the fulfilment of prophecy than in legal requirements, and to a breaking away from the Jewish emphasis on Torah; certainly it is consistent with the desire to show Jesus as the awaited, true Messiah.

As we might expect, the ways in which the New Testament writers use the Old Testament show the influence of the various contemporary Jewish methods of exegesis. Like the Rabbis, they quote the citation formula 'Scripture

says' (Matt. 4: 4, 6, 10; Rom. 10: 11), and Mark 2:
23–8 makes use of the Rabbinic practice of arguing 'a
minore ad maius' (from the lesser to the greater). From
the Old Testament story (1 Sam. 21: 1–6) of David's
followers breaking the regulations by eating the sacred
bread from the sanctuary the argument proceeds to a
justification of Jesus' disciples plucking and eating ears of
corn on the Sabbath, which would have been regarded as
contravening the principle of Sabbath observance. More
complicated is Rom. 4: 1–8, where Paul follows the
Rabbinic regulation regarding the association of verses
with a word or words in common – in this case the
word 'counted'. He quotes Gen. 15: 6, according to
which Abraham's faith was 'counted to him as righteousness', and asks what 'counted' means. In reply to his own
question he cites the reference in Ps. 32: 2 to the happiness
of the man whom God 'counts' as justified, and concludes from this that 'counting' in this sense is a matter of
free forgiveness and not of wages earned by good works.

In common with the Qumran literature, the New
Testament emphasizes the fulfilment of prophecy. In
particular, the author of the Gospel according to Matthew
frequently sees some event in the life of Jesus as having
been foretold in the Old Testament. For example,
Matt. 12: 16–21 claims that when Jesus 'gave strict
injunctions that they were not to make him known' he
was fulfilling Isa. 42: 1–3:

> He will not strive, he will not shout,
> nor will his voice be heard in the streets.

Nor is the influence of Hellenistic Judaism missing,
though it is perhaps not so easy to trace. It is sometimes
seen in the use of allegory, which seeks to bring out a

figurative meaning in details and words and phrases (unlike typology, which sees Old Testament stories and figures in a more general sense as figures or patterns which are repeated and summed up in Jesus Christ). Gal. 4 gives an extended allegorical interpretation of the Genesis story of Abraham and his two sons, Isaac and Ishmael. Graeco-Jewish thought may also have had a bearing on the treatment of the word 'true' in the Fourth Gospel, which owes something to Plato's notion (taken up and used by Philo) of the 'phenomenal' world of the things which we can see and touch and the 'real' world of abstract truth. In John 6: 31-3 the earthly manna eaten in the wilderness is a figure of the 'true' heavenly bread given by God in his Son.

These are only some of the methods which the New Testament writers employ when dealing with Old Testament material. What was their purpose in doing so? Here once more we find ideas in common with Judaism. With the Rabbis, they recognize the importance of tradition and try to use it to establish regulations for a consistent way of life. According to Acts 15: 16, 17 the crucial point in the debate as to whether or not Gentiles must be circumcised and undertake to keep the Law of Moses before being admitted to the Christian Church came when James quoted Amos 9: 11, 12:

> That they may seek the Lord – all the rest of mankind,
> and the Gentiles, whom I have claimed for my own.

2 Cor. 8: 15, setting out the principle of equality underlying the collection for the impoverished Jerusalem church, supports it by quoting the story of the gathering of the manna in the wilderness, 'The man who got much had no more than enough, and the man who got little did not go short.'

Again like the Qumran literature, the New Testament is anxious to demonstrate the fulfilment of prophecy, almost to the point of manipulating the Old Testament text. For example, Matt. 2: 18 applies Jer. 31: 15, the description of 'Rachel weeping for her children', to the massacre of the children by Herod the Great. Yet both the Qumran and the New Testament authors, however far-fetched at times their examples may seem, are deeply concerned to show that there is a real correspondence between prophecy and event. Because they are seen as theologically consistent at all times, God's words and acts in the past have something to say for the present and the future. This reason for interpreting the Old Testament afresh is common to the New Testament, Qumran, Rabbinic works and the writings of Philo.

But when we look further we see that there are basic differences between the Judaic and the New Testament interpretation and application of the Old Testament. For the Rabbis, the tradition of the past, stretching back to Mount Sinai (a claim which was made for the oral as well as for the written Law), was the final authority. This tradition supplies only a supporting framework for the New Testament; the real authority lies in the present. Paul can say, 'The tradition which I handed on to you came to me from the Lord himself' (1 Cor. 11: 23); Jesus declares, 'You have learned that our forefathers were told...But what I tell you is this' (Matt. 5: 21, 22). According to the Dead Sea Scrolls, the fulfilment of prophecy had still to reach its climax in the future, with the conflict between the 'children of light' and the 'children of darkness'. The New Testament sees the whole process of fulfilment, past, present and future, focused upon a single person, Jesus Christ, whose life, death and resurrection are events so decisive that all the rest of history can only be viewed as their subsequent working-out. Philo could only re-interpret an existing tradition in terms of hidden meanings in words and phrases. New Testament writers such as Paul and John move on to bear witness to a *new* act of God, and to produce a *New* Testament which can claim equality with the Old.

So for the authors of the New Testament the Old Testament has come to its climax of fulfilment in Jesus Christ; its prophecies find their ultimate meaning in him; its precepts, though good, are given a further dimension by the one who is 'the end of the law' (Rom. 10: 4, N.E.B. footnote). The same applies to its religious prac-tices. The Epistle to the Hebrews examines the sacrificial system, not suggesting that it was wrong in its insistence that man must be ceremonially clean before he can approach God, but showing that the work of Christ has done what the system could not do, by dealing with sin once and for all, and making free and confident access to God possible. 'So now, my friends', writes the author, 'the blood of Jesus makes us free to enter boldly into the sanctuary by the new, living way which he has opened for us through the curtain, the way of his flesh' (Heb. 10: 19, 20). The pattern of sacrifice need no longer be repeated.

All this raises problems. Paul, writing of the Law as 'a kind of tutor in charge of us until Christ should come', says, 'Now that faith has come, the tutor's charge is at an end' (Gal. 3: 24, 25), showing himself aware of these problems whilst wisely not attempting to solve them. Are we then to understand that the Old Testament, having done its work in preparing for and helping to support the new revelation, can be discarded? As we shall see, Marcion, a Christian writer of the second century, came to this very conclusion; not so the New Testament authors. Of course, in so far as they were Jews their reverence for the scriptures would be deep and lasting, but this is not the whole story. They see the relationship between the Testaments as something essentially two-way; not only does the Old support and explain the New, it is itself illuminated by what is revealed in Christ. In the Sermon on the Mount, it is not simply that the new precepts are better than the old: they bring to light what the old laws really meant. So alongside his 'But what I tell you is this' (Matt. 5: 22), Jesus can claim, 'Do not suppose that I have come to abolish the Law and the prophets; I did not come to abolish, but to complete' (Matt. 5: 17).

The Fourth Gospel takes this idea a step further. Not only does Jesus complete the Old Testament revelation, he is actually to be found within its pages. If, as the Lamb of God and the good shepherd (John 1: 29, 10: 14) he fulfils the images of sacrificial lamb and shepherd-king, these images must all the time in some sense have been speaking of him, even though this can only be appreciated retrospectively in the light of the New Testament author's later knowledge of his life and death. Commenting on Isa. 6: 10, 'He has blinded their eyes and dulled their minds, lest they should see with their eyes, and perceive with their minds, and turn to me to heal them', John 12: 41 says boldly, 'Isaiah said this because he saw his [Jesus'] glory and spoke about him.' Not every one will wholly agree with this kind of exegesis, but we must recognize that it expresses a belief in the continuing worth of the Old Testament in its own right and not simply as an introduction to the New.

The Old Testament and the early Church

For something like a hundred and fifty years after the resurrection, whilst the New Testament was being written and becoming known, most Christian exegesis dealt with the Old Testament, and was still influenced by Jewish thinking. Christian teachers faced the same problems as the New Testament writers in relation to the Jewish scriptures, and used much the same methods in attempting to solve them. The Epistle of Barnabas (about A.D. 130) produces a 'Christian' allegorization of the food laws in the Pentateuch; Justin Martyr (died A.D. 163), himself a Jew, finds 'types' of Christ in many of the Old Testament stories (among them the Ark, the exodus and the Passover lamb), and uses proof-texts in support of his more allegorical interpretations. For example, almost any reference to a staff, such as Aaron's staff (Exod. 7: 10), or the log which Moses threw into the bitter water at Marah (Exod. 15:25), or the 'staff and crook' of Ps. 23:4, prefigures the cross.

But already by Justin's time there had been great changes in the Christian community. In the first place, the Old Testament had been joined by the New, which had achieved a position of authority even though there was as yet nothing like an officially-recognized list of books. In the second place, although the influence of Judaism was to be permanent, the actual membership of the Church was now and would remain predominantly Gentile. The new generation of Christians and their successors, with Hellenistic rather than Jewish backgrounds, would need to appraise not only the attitude of the New Testament to the Old, but also the Old Testament in its own right, without any presuppositions.

It is of course impossible to do justice to the vast amount of literature on the subject produced by the Fathers (as the Christian scholars of the first five centuries are usually called); all that we can do is examine a few representative ideas. Nor must it be thought that in these early centuries once-and-for-all decisions were taken; discussion about the Old Testament continues to this day and is likely to do so indefinitely. Nevertheless, from the second half of the second century certain attitudes began to emerge which foreshadowed, and even reappeared in, later schools of thought.

An early challenge to both Testaments came from Marcion, a wealthy shipowner from Sinope on the shores of the Black Sea, who made his way to Rome in about A.D. 140, and undeterred by excommunication four years later propagated his views and organized his followers with maximum vigour and considerable effect until his death in A.D. 160. Marcion's central affirmation sounds curiously modern; he believed that the gospel was a gospel of love to the absolute exclusion of law. Therefore the New Testament was in no sense a continuation of the Old, but a protest against it. The Old Testament must be abandoned; its God was from the start a God of Law, cruel, fickle and despotic. Marcion uses the term 'Demiurge', from the Greek *demiourgos* = 'craftsman'. He shared this name and idea with Gnosticism (from the Greek *gnosis* meaning 'knowledge'), a complex religious movement which appears in 'Christian' form in the second century. Amongst other views it held that any form of matter was evil, therefore by definition a creating God could not be spiritual or good. Like others after him, Marcion found that to reject the Old Testament involved him in considerable difficulty with the New. He came to the conclusion that only Paul understood the essential difference between law and love, so his New Testament 'canon' consisted of ten Pauline epistles and a severely censored version of the Gospel according to Luke, chosen presumably because Luke was a Gentile and a friend of Paul.

If we are tempted to dismiss Marcion as an extremist without real importance we need only look at the calibre of the men who took the trouble to oppose his views during two hundred years or more of controversy. Here we can mention only three: Irenaeus, Tertullian and Origen.

Irenaeus (about A.D. 130–200), bishop of Lyons and an early influence in Western Christianity, was one of the first to take up the cudgels against him. His counter-attack was along two lines, not always entirely consistent with each other. On the one hand he was able to see biblical revelation as a timeless process, all bearing witness to the same truth. So essentially his view of the Old Testament was that of the Epistle to the Hebrews: 'When in former times God spoke to our forefathers, he spoke in fragmentary and varied fashion through the prophets. But in this the final age he has spoken to us in the Son whom he has made heir to the whole universe, and through whom he created all orders of existence' (Heb. 1: 1, 2). But on the other hand, to say that God spoke in 'fragmentary and varied fashion' in the Old Testament did not altogether answer the attacks of Marcion and the Gnostics upon the moral and theological soundness of such stories as the plagues of Egypt (Exod. 7–12) or the plundering of the Egyptians by the departing Israelites (Exod. 12: 35, 36). Irenaeus met these with what is sometimes called his theory of *progressive education*; the Old Testament was a record of the moral and spiritual education of the people of Israel and proceeded at a pace divinely ordered to fit their developing capacities. This has, of course, much in common with later ideas about progressive revelation, but to work out its full implications in this way would no doubt have conflicted with Irenaeus' equally firmly-held conviction that all revelation in the Bible is one, standing above the limitations of time.

Tertullian (about A.D. 155–225), a lawyer from Carthage in North Africa, and the first Father to write in Latin, argues against Marcion in his book *Adversus Marcionem*. His method was to read the Old Testament in as straightforward a way as possible, reducing allegory to a minimum, and he counters Marcion by picking out Old Testament passages to show that the Jesus of the Gospels is identical with the Messiah whom the prophets foretold. Every verse which seems to predict the events of Jesus' life and his death and his rejection by the Jews is pressed into service; the approach obviously has much in common with Justin Martyr's proof-texts.

Origen (A.D. 185–254) was probably the greatest of Marcion's critics and indeed one of the greatest Christian scholars of all time. He was a native of Alexandria, and for many years head of its Catechetical School, which nowadays we would describe as a Christian university specializing in biblical and theological studies. Origen was such a prolific writer that we cannot do more than look briefly at his attitude to the Old Testament. His *Hexapla* (see p. 150) is proof that he cared about preserving its text and finding the best translation, but how did he deal with matters of interpretation? He argued that just as in man there is body, soul and spirit, so in scripture there are three meanings – literal, moral and spiritual. He was quite prepared to defend the literal sense. When

Apelles, a disciple of Marcion, remarked that on the dimensions given in Genesis Noah's ark would just about have accommodated four elephants and their food, Origen replied, not too convincingly, that everything was all right if one squared the measurements. But his great interest lay in interpretation in the spiritual sense; for him the ark was primarily a symbol of the Christian church – in which men of reason were in a minority! He used allegory a great deal; not the rather cautious allegory of his predecessors, which specifically tried to make the Old Testament fit with Christian events and doctrines, but a wide-ranging kind of allegory which owed more to Philo than to Rabbinic or previous Christian thought. Meanings were drawn out of Old Testament, and for that matter New Testament, passages which had the most general moral, psychological and philosophical significance.

The effect upon biblical studies was profound. The 'proof-text' method went out of fashion, and in its place came the commentary, which undertook to comment in detail upon every word or phrase and to extract meaning from it. Origen claimed that this method went back to the Old Testament writers themselves; Ps. 78: 2:

> I will tell you a story with a meaning,
> I will expound the riddle of things past

he interprets as saying that the Psalmist had seen a deeper, hidden meaning in the events of the exodus which were about to be recounted.

Of course this brought its dangers: working without any strict terms of reference makes it very easy to read almost anything one wishes into a passage. Origen's opponents were not slow to accuse him of subjectivity, and there is truth in their criticism. But on the positive side, his breadth of outlook allied to his formidable intellect had a lasting and liberating influence upon the study of the Old Testament and indeed of the whole Bible.

So far it rather looks as if the Christian thinker of the first few centuries had only two alternatives as regards the Old Testament. Either he could reject it out of hand like Marcion, or in some way, whether by the use of proof-texts or typology or allegorization or a mixture of all three, he could read into it a series of pronouncements which related to something else, usually the New Testament. Had no-one any interest in it for its own sake?

It must be admitted that the view of the Old Testament as the source of innumerable oracles speaking of divine mysteries was popular; for one thing it was in line with fashionable ideas, which inclined away from the material and towards the mysterious. But alongside it there were more down-to-earth attempts at interpretation. Characters were used as examples of good and bad behaviour (it is unfortunate that Job was almost unanimously chosen as a model of patience, rather than of endurance, a piece of mis-casting which has persisted ever since). The Psalms were used in worship as was probably originally intended, and some of the 'wisdom' sayings were quoted for admonition and edification.

A change of emphasis from the preoccupation of Origen and other Alexandrian scholars with allegory – perhaps even a reaction against it, although the contrast must not be overstressed – can be seen in the work of the school of biblical scholarship which centred on Antioch in Syria during the fourth century and after. Its main interests were textual and historical; it looked not for hidden meanings but for the sense which the writers had intended in the first place. Consequently it was prepared to admit that some parts of the Bible were of greater value than others. Its two greatest exponents, John Chrysostom (about A.D. 347–407), and Theodore of Mopsuestia (about A.D. 350–428, see p. 63), were respectively a great preacher and a gifted commentator. John Chrysostom's seven hundred or more recorded sermons take the line of sober, historical exegesis, and we gather from his own comments that despite his gifts ('Chrysostom' means 'golden-mouthed') congregations sometimes found his preaching heavy going. It seems that one of his difficulties was that of relating the text to contemporary issues; allegorization did this so much more easily, and, however unfairly, was so much more fun.

Theodore of Mopsuestia (nicknamed 'the Interpreter' by posterity) has left behind commentaries on the Psalms and the minor prophets. In his work on the Psalms he tries to reconstruct from historical evidence the likeliest occasion for each Psalm's composition. He attributes them all to David, and where they speak of something which obviously happened after David's time suggests that David must have been gifted with prophetic prevision. On one matter he stands firm: only three Psalms (2, 8 and 45) make any reference to Jesus Christ, otherwise the Psalter is limited to the pre-Christian era. He takes the same line with the minor prophets; he is willing to see Amos' prophecies as referring to the future exile and return as well as to the Assyrian threat, but for him they do not point forward to Christ. He sees the break between the Testaments as absolute, typifying the break between the two periods which we now call B.C. and A.D. The Old Testament has its place in the over-all divine plan, but it is a historically and theologically restricted place.

It is tempting to overstress the likenesses between the Fathers and the twentieth century – to recognize Marcion's modern counterparts or to identify Theodore with the literary and historical critic. To do so is to do less than justice to the facts. The Fathers were men of their time who wrote against a background of culture and controversy which was very different from ours. Then, too, between them and us lie centuries of thought and scholarship: the mediaeval debates on the 'senses' – literal and spiritual – of the interpretation of scripture, and then the concern in the sixteenth century with the translation of the Bible into the vernacular. Erasmus wrote: 'I wish that the husbandman might sing parts of (the scriptures) at the plough: that the weaver may warble them at his shuttle: that the traveller may with their narratives beguile the weariness of the way'; similarly William Tyndale: 'If God spare my life ere many years I will cause a boy that driveth the plough to know more of the Scripture than thou dost.' Martin Luther, in his 'open letter' about translation, wrote, 'Sometimes for three and four weeks we have sought and asked for a single word and sometimes we have not found it even then. In working at the book of Job, Master Phillip, Aurogallus and I could sometimes scarcely finish three lines in four days.'

The insistence of the Reformers on the authority and living truth of this now 'open' Bible was followed in due course by the reaction of seventeenth- and eighteenth-century 'rational' thinking. This on the one hand tended to reduce interpretation of the scriptures to a sometimes rather superficial moralizing, but on the other hand, by the very detachment of its approach in the work of men such as Hobbes, Spinoza, Grotius and Astruc (see p. 64), marked the beginning of the type of biblical criticism which gained momentum and came to its climax during the nineteenth and early twentieth centuries. Add to all this the work of more recent scholarship, and the long tradition of Jewish thought with its vital and distinctive contribution to biblical studies, and we realize that we, in common with every age, must work out our own approach to the Bible in the light of our inheritance from the past as well as of contemporary knowledge and circumstances.

Yet some of the problems with which the Fathers wrestled are still with us. The relationship of the Old Testament to the New, the question of its value as literature in its own right, the inconvenient presence in its pages of material which for one reason or another is not easily explained – all these are matters which still concern us. If we are wise, we shall see that there is much to be learned from the approach of the past to these questions, even if we cannot always agree with its answers.

The Old Testament today

What place has the Old Testament in Christian thinking today? Of course, the Bible as a whole is and for centuries has been accorded special status by the Church. Christians are far from agreeing as to the exact nature of this status, but they hold in common the belief that the Bible reveals something of the essential nature and character of God, and that therefore in some sense it carries authority. Whether or not the reader thinks these beliefs are justified, he must accept the fact of their existence.

But within this framework is the Old Testament a kind of second-class work, outmoded and outdated by the New? We have seen how the New Testament writers themselves faced this problem and found no easy solution, and we have also seen something of the extent to which any understanding of the New Testament is dependent upon a knowledge and understanding of the Old. The quotations are only part of the story; there are many passages where Old Testament material is woven into the argument without anyone mentioning the fact. For example, Eph. 4: 25, 26: 'speak the truth to each other...If you are angry, do not let anger lead you into sin; do not let sunset find you still nursing it; leave no loop-hole for the devil', draws upon Zech. 8: 16: 'speak the truth to each other, administer true and sound justice in the city gate', and upon Ps. 4: 4:

> However angry your hearts, do not do wrong;
> though you lie abed resentful, do not break silence,

but we have to find this out for ourselves. Or what could we make of Rom. 3: 25: 'For God designed him to be the means of expiating sin by his sacrificial death, effective through faith' if we knew nothing of the sacrificial system; or of those who in Heb. 11: 39 are 'commemorated for their faith' if we could not look up their stories in the Old Testament and in other writings in the Apocrypha and elsewhere? Marcion at least was honest when he admitted that to ignore the Old Testament meant deleting a great deal of the New.

In Christian worship Old Testament influence is also apparent. Protestant churches regularly give a full place to Old Testament readings; in the Anglican tradition it provides one of the two readings in Morning and Evening Prayer, and the Apocrypha also has a place in the lectionaries. Psalms 95, 100, 98 and 67 are sung as Canticles, and the Benedicite comes from the 'Song of the Three' in the Apocrypha inserted in the Septuagint between

Dan. 3: 23 and 3: 24 as the song which the 'three faithful Jews' sang in the blazing furnace. Most of the versicles and responses are Old Testament quotations; for example,

> O Lord, open thou our lips:
> And our mouth shall shew forth thy praise

comes from Ps. 51: 15, and

> O Lord, shew thy mercy upon us:
> And grant us thy salvation

from Ps. 85: 7.

Over the centuries the Greek Orthodox and the Western Churches restricted the readings in the service of Holy Communion to the New Testament except on special occasions, but Exod. 20: 3–17 has supplied the Ten Commandments and Isa. 6: 3 the Sanctus: 'Holy, holy, holy, Lord God of hosts, heaven and earth are full of thy glory.' It is also interesting to note that recent liturgical revisions often give a greater place to the Old Testament.

Through the Jewish synagogue we are indebted to the Old Testament for the place of the Psalms in worship, and with metrical versions and hymn paraphrases they are used much more than is immediately obvious. To jettison the Old Testament would mean jettisoning

> The Lord's my shepherd, I'll not want,
> He makes me down to lie
> In pastures green; He leadeth me
> The quiet waters by

and

> All people that on earth do dwell,
> Sing to the Lord with cheerful voice:
> Him serve with fear, his praise forth tell
> Come ye before him and rejoice

and many others like them.

It would also mean a radical revision of other hymnology. 'The God of Abraham praise', and 'Holy, holy, holy, Lord God almighty' would be early casualties, as would

> Paschal Lamb ! Thine offering finished,
> Once for all, when Thou wast slain,
> In its fulness undiminished
> Shall for evermore remain.
> Alleluia, Alleluia,
> Cleansing souls from every stain,

and the following verses beginning

> Great High Priest of our profession,
> Through the veil thou enteredst in

and

> Life-imparting heavenly manna,
> Stricken rock, with streaming side.

We may, of course, argue that we can and do get on very well without some of the more obviously 'Old Testament flavoured' hymns; Isaac Watts'

> Not all the blood of beasts
> On Jewish altars slain,
> Could give the guilty conscience peace
> Or wash away the stain

is hardly fashionable at the moment. But we can argue even more strongly that we should be immeasurably the poorer if we lost them all.

Moving away from Christianity in its strictly confessional sense, it is often said that the Bible is part of the foundation of what is loosely called our 'Christian culture'. In this the Old Testament has had and still has its part. *Paradise Lost* is still read, Handel's *Israel in Egypt* and Benjamin Britten's *Noye's Fludde* are still performed,

Rembrandt's paintings of Tobias and Susanna are still famous. (See also *Old Testament Illustrations*, by C. M. Jones.) Even the 'biblical epics' of the screen, deplorable as some of them may be, frequently owe their origin, however distant, to stories such as the exodus or David and Bathsheba or Samson and Delilah. In the sphere of morality, the forbidding of murder, adultery and theft and the encouragement of kindness, truth-telling and promise-keeping are not exclusively biblical, but we should not underestimate the effectiveness of the Commandments and the prophetic teaching as a means of communicating these precepts to western man.

So the Christian Church by and large accepts the Old Testament, or parts of it, as essential to an understanding of Christian doctrine as expounded in the New Testament and as having an integral place in worship and even in 'Christian' culture in a wider sense. Are we then to conclude that it has no intrinsic worth except as forerunner and handmaid to Christianity? Let us look back at the different ways in which it can be studied (chapter 2); the determination of the 'best' text, the attempts to find the original life-situation of the literature, the history of its preservation and transmission and final editing, the comparison with the surviving literature of contemporary cultures. Clearly one of the uses to which all this can be put is the further illumination and elucidation of the New Testament, but is it the only use? Or, to return to the question which we asked ourselves at the beginning of this chapter, has the Old Testament in itself any relevance for the twentieth century?

It presents very real difficulties, as its detractors are not slow to point out. A great deal of its historicity or non-historicity cannot be proved or disproved. We shall in all probability never be able to reconstruct with certainty and exactitude the course of those key events, the exodus and wilderness wanderings and the Babylonian captivity and return. And then we still have to cope somehow with 'The LORD made Pharaoh obstinate' (Exod. 9: 12) and

> Happy is he who shall seize your children
> and dash them against the rock (Ps. 137: 9)

and many other awkward passages. Can current Old Testament study help us with these and similar problems? We can only answer fully for ourselves if we are willing to engage in this study; but here are some preliminary points for consideration.

First, if an event can be proved to have taken place it shows that the writer was not a romancer or an out-and-out liar. But does it help prove the validity of the interpretation which is placed on this event? For example, if the exact date of the exodus, the exact numbers of people involved and the exact route or routes taken were by some means known without a shadow of doubt, would it help us to any deeper understanding of what Jeremiah meant when he said

These are the words of the LORD:

> I remember the unfailing devotion of your youth,
> the love of your bridal days,
> when you followed me in the wilderness,
> through a land unsown (Jer. 2: 2)?

Conversely, if a narrative can be clearly shown to be historically inaccurate, it does not mean that we automatically discard it; we still have other questions to ask about its meaning. Perhaps after all the question of historical 'truth' is not always as vitally important as we think, since there are also other kinds of truth.

Secondly, if we are to understand Old Testament thought we must see it in the context of its time and environment. The Torah in its entirety may not meet the requirements of modern society, but we can compare it with other contemporary legal provisions. As we have seen earlier, archaeological discovery can do much to help us towards this understanding.

Thirdly, if we are prepared to accept that the Old Testament in any way sets out to be a record of God's revelation of himself to man, we must also be prepared to accept that the revelation is hardly likely to have been made completely and simultaneously; it is far more probable that it was a lengthy and continuing process. And there is the further possibility that where there was a wrong or inadequate response there was in due time a further revelation to correct this response. The process has been likened to a dialogue between God and man – intermittent, and impeded by foolishness and stupidity and even wilful disobedience on man's part, but a continuing dialogue all the same. The book of Job goes so far as to set out its contents in this way, with Job and his three friends all joining in with a will, and being answered and corrected by Yahweh. In fact the Old Testament, unlike other religious books, is a commentary on the religious growth of a community, following it through its trials and sorrows, its joys and awakenings. So it can have relevance to the similar problems of any growing nation. If we want to know about religion, which is an aspect of human experience, we will do well to look here. But this is not all. The scriptures themselves and the continuing interpretation of them have helped to form two living religions, Judaism and Christianity. At the same time, the experiences of these communities, historically and in their cultural relationships, have helped to formulate the interpretation. This constant and continuing interaction is a sign of a tradition which is very much alive.

Above all we must keep a sense of proportion and realize that not all the Old Testament and Apocrypha are what we are pleased to call 'sub-Christian' or crude or primitive. In spite of their age and all their difficulties they speak of a kind of experience which we can instantly recognize. The view of human nature is realistic; Moses' diffidence, his family's jealousy, David's disastrous domestic life, Jeremiah's agonized self-doubt, Daniel's obstinate courage, Ben Sirach's shrewd common sense, leaving aside any critical problems which surround them, all have a familiar ring. And has the picture of God himself anything to say to us? He is transcendent in majesty yet near at hand:

> Thus speaks the high and exalted one,
> whose name is holy, who lives for ever:
> I dwell in a high and holy place
> with him who is broken and humble in spirit,
> to revive the spirit of the humble,
> to revive the courage of the broken (Isa. 57: 15).

He demands the very highest standards of behaviour:

> God has told you what is good;
> and what is it that the LORD asks of you?
> Only to act justly, to love loyalty,
> to walk wisely before your God (Mic. 6: 8),

yet he is compassionate and forgiving:

I have swept away your sins like a dissolving mist,
and your transgressions are dispersed like clouds (Isa. 44: 22).

These, and so many other passages, have a claim to timeless authority and a place among 'the lively oracles of God'.

SUGGESTIONS FOR FURTHER READING

B. J. BAMBERGER *The Bible: a Modern Jewish Approach*, New York, 1963.

J. BOWDEN *What about the Old Testament?*, London, 1969.

C. H. DODD *According to the Scriptures*, London, 1952.

A. HERZBERG *Judaism*, London and New York, 1961.

D. E. NINEHAM (ed.) *The Church's Use of the Bible, Past and Present*, London, 1963.

W. W. SIMPSON *Jewish Prayer and Worship*, London, 1965.

INDEX OF REFERENCES

GENERAL INDEX